"Everything Kevin DeYoung writes is biblical, timely, and helpful for both life and ministry. You can't afford to miss what he says here in *Crazy Busy*. He rightly reminds us to beware of the barrenness of a busy life, since activity and productivity are not the same thing."

Rick Warren, #1 *New York Times* best-selling author,
The Purpose Driven Life; Pastor, Saddleback Church

"I'm a fan of Kevin DeYoung's writing, partly because I know what to expect. He's always clear, biblical, and to the point—with a good dose of humor peppered in. *Crazy Busy* is no exception. It's a quick and engaging read that busy people can find time for. DeYoung helped me think about the heart issues behind my busyness, and even gave me some practical ways to fight it. As a pretty busy guy, I encourage other busy folks to squeeze this little book into their schedule."

Trip Lee, hip-hop artist; author, *The Good Life*

"A great book for the stressed-out. DeYoung shows that Jesus was busy and Christians should be busy discipling nations, parenting children, and bearing burdens. He rightly differentiates that from 'crazy busy,' a frenzied trying to please some and control others—and he shows how biblical rhythms and trust in God's providence can keep us sane. Also a great book for parents who live in a Kindergarchy, over-programming their children: DeYoung says let them play, because it's not easy either to ruin them or to assure their success."

Marvin Olasky, Editor-in-chief, World News Group

"I'm glad to take time out of my busy life to endorse *Crazy Busy* by Kevin DeYoung. As Kevin makes abundantly clear, our busyness can be evidence of our faithfulness or, on the other hand, evidence of our pride, ambition, and unbridled activity. As always, Kevin DeYoung is a careful thinker, a gifted pastor, and a writer who keeps us on the edge of our seat."

R. Albert Mohler Jr., President and Joseph Emerson Brown
Professor of Christian Theology, The Southern Baptist
Theological Seminary

"Habitual, sinful busyness is something that many struggle with and yet, it's rare to hear teaching on this important topic. With refreshing transparency and his trademark humor, Kevin DeYoung identifies the problem and gives helpful practical instruction on how to find our rest in Christ. DeYoung has served the church well (once again). I highly recommend this book."

Shai Linne, hip-hop artist

CRAZY
BUSY

CRAZY
BUSY

A (MERCIFULLY) SHORT BOOK ABOUT A (REALLY) BIG PROBLEM

KEVIN DEYOUNG

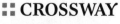

CROSSWAY

WHEATON, ILLINOIS

Crazy Busy: A (Mercifully) Short Book about a (Really) Big Problem

Copyright © 2013 by Kevin DeYoung

Published by Crossway
    1300 Crescent Street
    Wheaton, Illinois 60187

Published in association with the literary agency of Wolgemuth & Associates, Inc.

Cover design: Faceout Studio

First printing 2013

Printed in the United States of America

Unless otherwise indicated, Scripture quotations are from the ESV® Bible (*The Holy Bible, English Standard Version*®), copyright © 2001 by Crossway. 2011 Text Edition. Used by permission. All rights reserved.

The Scripture reference marked "NIV" is taken from The Holy Bible, New International Version®, NIV®. Copyright © 1973, 1978, 1984, 2011 by Biblica, Inc.™ Used by permission. All rights reserved worldwide.

The Scripture reference marked "the Message" is from *The Message*. Copyright © by Eugene H. Peterson 1993, 1994, 1995, 1996, 2000, 2001, 2002. Used by permission of NavPress Publishing Group.

The Scripture quotation marked "KJV" is from the King James Version of the Bible.

Trade paperback ISBN: 978-1-4335-3338-9
PDF ISBN: 978-1-4335-3339-6
Mobipocket ISBN: 978-1-4335-3340-2
ePub ISBN: 978-1-4335-3341-9

Library of Congress Cataloging-in-Publication Data

DeYoung, Kevin.
 Crazy busy : a (mercifully) short book about a (really)
big problem / Kevin DeYoung.
   pages cm
 Includes bibliographical references and index.
 ISBN 978-1-4335-3338-9
 1. Time management—Religious aspects—Christianity.
I. Title.
BV4598.5.D49   2013
650.1'1—dc23   2013005889

Crossway is a publishing ministry of Good News Publishers.

LB			23	22	21	20	19	18	17	16	15
16	15	14	13	12	11	10	9	8	7	6	5

To Mark, Lig, C. J., Al, Thabiti, Matt,
John, and David, busy friends,
who have made time for me.

Contents

Hello, My Name Is Busy

I am the worst possible person to write this book.

And maybe the best.

My life is crazy busy. I don't say that as a boast or a brag. I'm not trying to win any contest. I'm just stating the facts. Or at least describing the way my life feels almost every single day. I often made the quip, "I'm supposed to write a book on busyness, if only I could find the time." And I wasn't joking.

How did I get this way? How did you get this way? How did we all get this way? I've yet to meet anyone in America who responds to the question "How are you?" with the reply, "Well for starters, I'm not very busy." I suppose there must be a six-year-old somewhere out there who doesn't "have anything to do" and some dear folks at the nursing home who could use a few more interruptions, but for almost everyone in between there is a pervasive sense of being unrelentingly filled up and stressed out.

I do not write this book as one who has reached the summit and now bends over to throw the rope down to everyone else. More like the guy with a toehold three feet off the ground, looking for my next grip. I'm writing this book not because I know more than others but because I want to know more than I do. I want to know why life feels the way it does, why our world is the way it is, why I am the way I am. And I want to change.

Same Kind of Busy as You

As long as I can remember—which takes us back aeons and aeons, all the way to the 90s—I have been busy. In high school I ran track and cross-country, played intramural basketball, did National Honor Society, tried the Spanish club, took multiple AP courses, played in our insanely time-consuming marching band, sang in a musical, and did church twice on Sunday, Sunday school, youth group, and a Friday morning Bible study. No one made me like this. My parents didn't force me (though church was not up for discussion). I wanted to do all these things.

In college I did even more. I ran a season of track, played intramural sports, worked part-time for various professors, organized one of the country's largest Model UN programs (yes, it's true), signed up to be a DJ at the campus radio station, led our Fellowship of Christian Students group, went to voluntary chapel three times a week, sang in a church choir, sang in the college chapel choir, participated in my church's college ministry, helped with Boys' Brigade on Wednesday nights, went to church on Sunday morning, then Sunday school, then evening church, then chapel back on campus late into the night.

Same story in seminary. In addition to normal course work and wading through my denomination's labyrinthine ordination process, I interned at my church, preached regularly, sang in up to three different choirs at the same time, went to an accountability group every week, did the usual with church twice on Sunday, plus Sunday school, plus a midweek catechism class I taught for little kids, plus leading the seminary's missions committee and attending chapels and frequent prayer meetings. I could go on and on.

And this is before I was *really* busy. The only people busier than single grad students are people who aren't single and aren't grad students. All those years in school, except for one semester, I wasn't married. I wasn't in full-time pastoral ministry. I wasn't blogging or writing books. I wasn't leading elders' meetings. I wasn't speaking anywhere. I wasn't a slave to technology. I didn't have a mortgage to figure out or a lawn to mow or a furnace to fix or a dead raccoon in my fireplace (long story) or weekly sermons to prepare. I didn't have to travel. I didn't have Facebook or Twitter. Hardly anyone e-mailed me. And I wasn't parenting a child, let alone five.

On most days, my responsibilities, requirements, and ambitions add up to much more than I can handle. It has since I was a teenager, and only seems to be getting worse. When someone asks me how I'm doing, my response almost always includes the word "busy." I can think of several moments in just the past couple of months when I've muttered to myself, "What am I doing? How did I get myself into this mess? When will I ever get my life under control? How long can I keep this up? Why can't I manage my time? Why did I say yes to this? How did I get so busy?" I've bemoaned my poor planning and poor decision making. I've complained about my schedule. I've put in slipshod work because there wasn't time for any other kind. I've missed too many quiet times and been too impatient with my kids. I've taken my wife for granted and fed important relationships with leftovers. I've been too busy to pursue God with my whole heart, soul, mind, and strength.

In other words, I've likely been just like you.

An Idea Whose Time Was Overdue

"So, Kevin, what's your next book project?" my friends would ask.

"I'm doing a book on busyness."

"Really?! But your schedule is a mess. This is one of your biggest problems."

"I know. That's why I'm writing the book."

Some books are written because the author knows something people need to know. Others because the author has seen something people should see. I'm writing this book to figure out things I don't know and to work on change I have not yet seen. More than any other book I've worked on, this one is for me.

Which also means the book will have more about me than usual. I don't know any other way to write on a topic that has been such a personal struggle except to make this book very personal. There is nothing remarkable about my experiences such that they need to be shared. It just so happens they are the experiences I know best. So you're going to get a candid look at some of my faults, some of my struggles, and some of the insights—commonsense and biblical—that have helped me make sense of my heart issues.

I have two hesitations in writing a book like this, and both stem from pride. On the one hand, I'm going to put aside the urge to constantly qualify my struggles with reassurances that things aren't quite so bad as they sound. In one sense, that's true. I have a happy marriage and love being a dad. I'm not burnt out. I'm not fifty pounds overweight. I sleep at night. I have friends. There are people in my life to keep me accountable. This book is not a cry for help.

Except that it is. I want to grow in this area. I don't want to keep up this same pace for the rest of my life. Frankly, I probably can't. My life may not be spinning out of control, but it's probably spinning too fast and a bit wobbly.

My second hesitation is just the opposite. I worry that you'll think I'm parading my busyness as a badge of honor. If you don't think I'm messed up for having these issues in the first place, you might think I'm proud for talking about them at all. "Must be nice to speak at conferences, Rev Kev. Must be pretty sweet to have people asking you to write books. Nice name drop, Pastor—wish those guys were knocking down my door. Thanks for sharing all your *terrible* burdens with us."

I understand the sentiment. When some people talk about busyness it sounds like the lantern-jawed zillionaire quarterback complaining about all the photo shoots he has lined up. I really hope I don't sound like That Guy—the one who expects sympathy every time he tells his sob story about how much worse the Milan airport is compared to Prague. As far as I can discern my heart, I'm not proud to be busy and I'm not proud of the things that make me busy. To be sure, pride is connected in other ways, but not in the sharing of the struggles themselves.

Besides, when it comes down to it, we are all busy in the same sorts of ways. Whether you are a pastor, a parent, or a pediatrician, you likely struggle with the crushing weight of work, family, exercise, bills, church, school, friends, and a barrage of requests, demands, and desires. No doubt, some people are quantitatively less busy than others and some much more so, but that doesn't change the shared experience: most everyone I know feels frazzled and overwhelmed most of the time.

That's what the people in my church are like. That's what my friends around the country are like. That's what I am like. And that's why I'm writing this book.

Worlds Apart?

I read an anecdote once about a woman from another culture who came to the United States and began to introduce herself as "Busy." It was, after all, the first thing she heard when meeting any American. *Hello, I'm Busy*—she figured it was part of our traditional greeting, so she told everyone she met that that's who she was.

It's what most of us are, and what more of us are becoming. No matter where we live or what our background. Granted, there are important differences in how people understand time. I'm well aware that this book assumes a modernized, industrialized cultural context. I know it assumes a Western view of time, and that an African book on busyness might include different prescriptions and contain many insights I've missed. To that end, I trust you will distinguish in these pages between practical application (which may differ across cultures) and biblical principles and diagnoses (which do not). Efficiency and punctuality, for example, can demonstrate respect for others, but they are not absolute virtues. Just ask the man on the Jericho Road.

But we all live somewhere and must swim in the water around us. I can't help but deal with the realities of life as I experience them in the United States. While it may limit the effectiveness of this book in some contexts, it seemed best *not* to take off my Western lenses, both because I probably couldn't and because the world, for better or worse, will only grow more globalized, urbanized, and busy in the years ahead. Many other cultures are not as obsessed with minutes and seconds as we are, but for most of us, that's the world we inhabit. For the rest, it's the world that's coming.

Paint by Numbers

I hope you'll find this book highly practical and accessibly theological. That's the book I set out to write because that's the book I'd want to read. In these pages, I don't plumb the depths of union with Christ, eschatological foreshadowing, and the interpretive history of the fourth commandment. That's not the kind of book you're reading. At the same time, I'm not interested merely in giving time management techniques or tips on how to set your e-mail filter. I want to understand what's going on in the world and in my heart to make me feel the way I do. And I also want to understand how to change—even just a little. Both tasks require theology. And both are begging for practicality.

The outline of this book is straightforward. If you want a poem or a chalk drawing about busyness, you won't find it here. But if you prefer a clear outline with lists, I'm your man. My outline is as simple as three numbers: 3, 7, and 1: three dangers to avoid (chapter 2), seven diagnoses to consider (chapters 3–9), and one thing you must do (chapter 10). I don't promise total transformation. I offer no money-back guarantees. My goal is more modest. I hope you'll find a few ways to tackle your schedule, several suggestions for reclaiming your sanity, and a lot of encouragement to remember your soul.

All of which is to say, I hope you find in reading this book exactly what I'm looking for in writing it.

2

Here, There, and Gone: Three Dangers to Avoid

It's not the most famous story in the Bible, but it is one of the strangest. At the end of 1 Kings 20 we meet a man who comes up with an unusual plan for rebuking Israel's king. God's people were at war with Syria, and God was granting them military success. But Ahab was a wicked, petulant, cowardly king. Just when God gave the Syrian king, Ben-hadad, into his hands, Ahab agreed to let him go for a few bazaars in Damascus. The gesture may sound magnanimous to us, but Ahab's selfish little bargain put all of Israel in danger and dishonored the Lord.

So a certain man of the sons of the prophets devised a plan. He would go to the king dressed like a servant returning from battle. The first step was to look the part, so the unnamed prophet ordered a fellow prophet, at the command of the Lord, to strike him. Somewhat understandably, this second fellow did not oblige, which led to his untimely death at the hands of a lion (I told you it was a strange story). So the prophet found another man and also implored him, "Strike me, please." This time the man struck and wounded him.

Now the prophet was ready to go the king. Fresh with these self-inflicted bruises, the man disguised himself with a bandage over his eyes and told the king a story: "I've just come from the battle," he said, "and I need to tell you something. A soldier brought me a man and ordered me to guard him with my life. Well, one thing led to another, and I must have got distracted with something else and, um, the man got away."

Of course, the king was furious: "Just as you said: this negligence will cost you your life." Then the prophet removed the bandage, revealed his true identity, and rebuked the king for letting Ben-hadad go free when God wanted him dead. Not a smart move. Disobedience would cost Ahab his life, just as he ironically said it should.

My point in recounting this obscure incident is not to encourage you to punch each other in the face. I mention this story so we can underline what the prophet-turned-pretend-guard says to the king in explaining how his man got away: "And as your servant was busy here and there, he was gone" (1 Kings 20:40). I realize 1 Kings 20 is not trying to tackle the problem of busyness, but the line in verse 40 strikes me as a perfect description for our age. We are here and there and everywhere. We are distracted. We are preoccupied. We can't focus on the task in front of us. We don't follow through. We don't keep our commitments. We are so busy with a million pursuits that we don't even notice the most important things slipping away.

Confession Is Good for the Soul

You and I have a problem. Most mornings, we drag ourselves out of bed, start the day's routine, and hope against hope that we can simply hold our ground. Maybe we can keep the house in only a mild state of disaster. Maybe we can break even on the to-do list. Maybe no one else will get sick. Maybe the in-box won't get any fuller. Maybe we won't fall asleep after lunch. Maybe, just maybe, we can get enough done in the next eighteen hours to beat back the beast of busyness and live to see another day. We wake up most days not trying to serve, just trying to survive.

In his book *The Busy Christian's Guide to Busyness*, Tim Chester suggests twelve diagnostic questions to determine how ill we've become with "hurry sickness."[1] I can imagine how we'd answer each question in our church small groups. And then I can imagine how we'd *really* respond:

1. "Do you regularly work thirty minutes a day longer than your contracted hours?"
   What does that have to do with anything? I have a lot to do, so I have to work a lot of hours.

2. "Do you check work e-mails and phone messages at home?"
   Are you serious? Have you been around much this millennium?

3. "Has anyone ever said to you, 'I didn't want to trouble you because I know how busy you are'?"

---

[1] Tim Chester, *The Busy Christian's Guide to Busyness* (Nottingham, England: Inter-Varsity Press, 2006), 9–10.

Of course! And I'm glad they have the decency to respect my time!

4. "Do your family or friends complain about not getting time with you?"
   Well, I wouldn't call it complaining per se. They're still learning that quality time is more important than quantity time.

5. "If tomorrow evening were unexpectedly freed up, would you use it to do work or a household chore?"
   Uh, yeah. Were you going to do it for me?

6. "Do you often feel tired during the day or do you find your neck and shoulders aching?"
   Mountain Dew, ibuprofen, not a problem.

7. "Do you often exceed the speed limit while driving?"
   Depends on whether I'm trying to eat French fries at the same time.

8. "Do you make use of any flexible working arrangements offered by your employers?"
   Definitely. I work at home. I work in the car. I work on vacation. I can work pretty much anywhere.

9. "Do you pray with your children regularly?"
   I never turn them down when they ask.

10. "Do you have enough time to pray?"
    I'm more a "pray continually" kind of person. I don't need to set aside specific times to pray because I'm always in communion with God.

11. "Do you have a hobby in which you are actively involved?"
    Does Pinterest count?

12. "Do you eat together as a family or household at least once a day?"

More or less. When one person is eating, someone else is usually in the house at the same time.

On a normal day, my life feels like something between a perpetual summer camp and a three-ring circus. You probably feel the same. Think about the average workweek in this country. It wasn't that long ago we had futurists predicting that one of the main challenges for coming generations would be too much spare time. In 1967, for example, testimony before a Senate subcommittee claimed that by 1985 the average workweek would be just twenty-two hours.[2] Instead, Americans lead the industrialized world in annual work hours. Our annual hours have increased from 1,716 for the average worker in 1967 to 1,878 hours in the year 2000.[3] British workers put in an extra hour every day compared to the Germans and the Italians, but that's still almost an hour less than Americans.[4] If you want a little easier load (and a lot of oil-generated wealth), consider Norway. Workers there put in an average of 14 weeks fewer per year than their American counterparts.[5]

A Busy New World

It's perplexing when you think about it. Why should we—Americans, Westerners, almost anyone in the industrialized world—why should we, of all people, be so busy when we live in such luxury? Are we wimps? Are we bringing this

[2] Cited in Richard A. Swenson, *Margin: Restoring Emotional, Physical, Financial, and Time Reserves to Overloaded Lives* (Colorado Springs: NavPress, 2004), 114.
[3] Ibid., 115.
[4] Chester, *Busy Christian's Guide*, 10.
[5] Swenson, *Margin*, 115.

on ourselves? Are we especially poor at managing our lives? Maybe; it's possible; perhaps. But there does seem to be something unique about our time.

At first it seems like life couldn't possibly be more challenging in any way than, say, during the Reformation. A guy like John Calvin never had indoor plumbing. He didn't have centralized heat or air conditioning. He had to write his books and letters by hand or dictate them to a scribe. He had no automobile to get around in. His life had almost none of the comforts we take for granted. He was sick all the time. He worked too much. He died at 54. People can be busy in any century.

But while people can drive themselves to exhaustion in any age, there's no mistaking that sixteenth-century Geneva was a far simpler place than our world today. There are two realities of the modernized, urbanized, globalized world that most everyone else in human history could not fathom: *our complexity* and *our opportunity*. I could give you statistics about the terabytes of information on the Internet or the number of cereals at your grocery store to prove my point, but I don't have to. No one has to convince you that this is what the world is like.

We have more opportunity than ever before. The ability to cheaply go anywhere is a recent development. The ability to get information from anywhere is, too. Even the ability to easily stay up past sundown is relatively new. The result, then, is simple but true: because we *can* do so much, we *do* do so much. Our lives have no limits. We eat (most of) what we want, buy (most of) what we want, and say yes to (too much of) what we want. In all of our lifetimes we've seen an exponential expansion in the number of opportunities for children, opportunities for seniors, opportunities for leisure, opportunities for travel, opportunities for education, opportunities at church (and for different churches), opportunities in our local communities, and opportunities to make a difference around the world. No wonder we are so busy.

And alongside this explosion of opportunity in the modern world is a mind-boggling complexity. I went to Boston for seminary in 1999. Since my college was only twenty miles from where I grew up, seminary marked the first time I had been far away from home. The class work was challenging, but the real frustration that first year was figuring out how to be a grown-up. I planned out my reading and writing assignments meticulously, but no one told me to plan for all the exigencies of life. I had to figure out how to get my car fixed: where to take it, how to get there, and how to come up with $1,500 for a new transmission. I had to apply for financial aid. I had to navigate health insurance and car insurance. I had to open a new bank account. I had to do my own taxes. I had to get a phone set up and learn to pay my bills through a maze of automated instructions. I had to get a dial-up Internet connection. I had to do my own laundry, fold my own clothes, and iron my own shirts.[6] And like so many young people, I had to do all of this without any family around or any close friends to show me the ropes. I had never known such bewilderment as in that first year, trying to become a functioning adult in our complicated

---

[6] Yes, I know. This should have happened in college, but since I was so close to home I managed to get by for four years with doing almost no laundry.

world. Everything took time—time I didn't have, and time I didn't plan for. What a bother. What a pain.

I even got called for jury duty.

Three Dangers to Avoid

As hectic and frustrating as modern life can be, the biggest dangers are not material or temporal inconveniences. A person can do physical labor twelve hours a day, six days a week for an entire life and not suffer many ill effects. In fact, he or she may be healthier for it. But if the strain is mental—as is the case for most jobs and for most of us—the negative impact on the body can be huge.[7] So don't ignore the physical danger of busyness. Just remember the most serious threats are *spiritual*. When we are crazy busy, we put our souls at risk. The challenge is not merely to make a few bad habits go away. The challenge is to not let our spiritual lives slip away. The dangers are serious, and they are growing. And few of us are as safe as we may think.

The first danger is that busyness can ruin our joy. This is the most immediate and obvious spiritual threat. As Christians, our lives should be marked by joy (Phil. 4:4), taste like joy (Gal. 5:22), and be filled with the fullness of joy (John 15:11). Busyness attacks all of that. One study found that commuters experience greater levels of stress than fighter pilots and riot police.[8] That's what we're facing. When our lives are frantic and frenzied, we are more prone to anxiety, resentment, impatience, and irritability.

---

[7] Swenson, *Margin*, 46.
[8] Chester, *Busy Christian's Guide*, 115.

As I worked on this book, I could sense an improved spirit within me. Not because of my writing, but because of the time off I was granted to do the writing. During those weeks away from the pressures of travel, meetings, and constant sermon preparation, I found myself more patient with my kids, more thoughtful toward my wife, and more able to hear from God. Obviously, we all have weeks and months where everything that can go wrong does go wrong. In those seasons we will have to fight hard for joy in the midst of busyness. But few of us will fight *right now* for *next week's* joy by tackling the unnecessary habits of busyness that make most weeks an unhappy hassle.

Years ago I listened to an interview with Richard Swenson, a Christian physician, about the concept of "margin." There's nothing uniquely Christian about the idea itself, but there is something very un-Christian about ignoring it. "Margin," Swenson says, "is the space between our load and our limits."[9] Planning for margin means planning for the unplannable. It means we understand what's possible for us as finite creatures and then we schedule for *less* than that.

Over the past year I've come to see that I plan no margin in my weeks—reverse margin, actually. I look at my week, and before any interruptions come or any new opportunities arise or any setbacks occur, I already have no idea how to get everything done. I see the meetings scheduled, the sermons to be prepared, the e-mails I need to write, the blogs I need to post, the projects I need to complete, the people I need to see, and I figure that if everything goes a little better than expected, it

---

[9] Ibid., 69.

can all be squeezed in. But of course, there are no ideal weeks, and so I end up with no margin to absorb the surprises. So I hunker down, get harried, and get busy. That's all I can do in the moment because I didn't plan better weeks before.

Busyness is like sin: kill it, or it will be killing you. Most of us fall into a predictable pattern. We start to get overwhelmed by one or two big projects. Then we feel crushed by the daily grind. Then we despair of ever feeling at peace again and swear that something has to change. Then two weeks later life is more bearable, and we forget about our oath until the cycle starts all over again. What we don't realize is that all the while we've been a joyless wretch, snapping like a turtle and as personally engaging as a cat. When busyness goes after joy, it goes after everyone's joy.

The second danger is that busyness can rob our hearts. The sower tossed his seed liberally. Some fell along the path, and the birds devoured it. Some fell on rocky ground and sprang up quickly, only to wither away in the first scorching heat. And some fell among thorns, which choked out its fragile life. There's a definite progression in Jesus's parable (Mark 4:1–20). In some hearts, the Word of God does nothing. Satan scoops it up as soon as it is sown. In other hearts, the Word grows at first and then fades just as fast. Persecutions and trials put the would-be Christian out of commission. But in the third category of unsuccessful soil the Word sinks in a little deeper. The plant sprouts up, almost to the point of producing fruit. It looks a lot like good soil. New life seems to be taking root. Everything is on track for the harvest. Until the thorns come.

John Calvin says the human heart is "a thick forest of thorns."[10] Jesus names two in particular. The first he labels "the cares of the world" (Mark 4:19). Do you know why retreats and mission trips and summer camps and Christian conferences are almost always good for your spiritual growth? Because you have to clear your schedule to do them. You get away. You set aside your normal insanity for a weekend and find the space to think, pray, and worship.

For most of us, it isn't heresy or rank apostasy that will derail our profession of faith. It's all the worries of life. You've got car repairs. Then your water heater goes out. The kids need to see a doctor. You haven't done your taxes yet. Your checkbook isn't balanced. You're behind on thank you notes. You promised your mother you'd come over and fix a faucet. You're behind on wedding planning. Your boards are coming up. You have more applications to send out. Your dissertation is due. Your refrigerator is empty. Your lawn needs mowing. Your curtains don't look right. Your washing machine keeps rattling. This is life for most of us, and it's choking out spiritual life.

A second thorn is related to the first. Jesus says the work of the Word is swallowed up by the desire for other things. It's not that possessions themselves are to blame. The problem is with everything we do to take care of them and everything we do to get more of them. Is it any wonder that the most stressed-out people on the planet live in the most affluent countries? Cottages, boats, campers, time-shares, investments, real estate, snowmobiles, new cars, new houses, new computers,

---

[10] John Calvin, *Commentary on a Harmony of the Evangelists*, vol. 2 (Grand Rapids, MI: Eerdmans, 1949), 116.

new iStuff, new video games, new makeup, new DVDs, new downloads, new . . . —they all take time. We've heard countless sermons warning us about the dangers of money. But the real danger comes after you spend the money. Once you own it you need to keep it clean, keep it working, and keep up with the latest improvements. If the worries of life don't swamp us, the upkeep will.

Jesus knows what he's talking about. As much as we must pray against the Devil and pray for the persecuted church, in Jesus's thinking the greater threat to the gospel is sheer exhaustion. Busyness kills more Christians than bullets. How many sermons are stripped of their power by lavish dinner preparations and professional football? How many moments of pain are wasted because we never sat still enough to learn from them? How many times of private and family worship have been crowded out by soccer and school projects? We need to guard our hearts. The seed of God's Word won't grow to fruitfulness without pruning for rest, quiet, and calm.

The third danger is that busyness can cover up the rot in our souls. The hectic pace of life can make us physically and spiritually sick. That's not likely a surprise to you. What we may not recognize is that our crazy schedules are often signals that the sickness has already set in.

Since 2002 I've gotten together each fall with my friends from seminary. Nine of us met every week while we were at Gordon-Conwell, and when we graduated we made a commitment to see each other once a year. We eat a lot, laugh a lot, and watch a lot of football. We also talk about our joys and struggles from the past twelve months. Over the years we've noticed familiar themes for each of us. One guy may typically struggle with discontentment, another with discouragement, another with direction, another with relational strains at work. We all have our besetting sins and predictable issues. Mine has been busyness. When it comes time for me to share, everyone expects to hear how I have too much to do and don't know what to cut out of my life.

While it may sound unhealthy for grown men to wrestle with the same issues year after year, the healthy sign is that we've begun to take more responsibility for our struggles. We realize that if the same issues smack the same guys every year, then maybe the real issue is inside each of us. What does it say about me that I'm frequently overwhelmed? What do I need to learn about myself? What biblical promises am I not believing? What divine commands am I ignoring that I should obey? What self-imposed commands am I obeying that I should ignore? What's going on in my soul, so that busyness comes out as my chief challenge every year?

The presence of extreme busyness in our lives may point to deeper problems—a pervasive people-pleasing, a restless ambition, a malaise of meaninglessness. "Busyness serves as a kind of existential reassurance, a hedge against emptiness," writes Tim Kreider in his viral article, "The 'Busy' Trap," for the *New York Times*. "Obviously your life cannot possibly be silly or trivial or meaningless if you are so busy, completely booked, in demand every hour of the day."[11] The greatest danger with

---

[11] Tim Kreider, "The 'Busy' Trap," *New York Times*, June 30, 2012.

busyness is that there may be greater dangers you never have time to consider.

Busyness does not mean you are a faithful or fruitful Christian. It only means you are busy, just like everyone else. And like everyone else, your joy, your heart, and your soul are in danger. We need the Word of God to set us free. We need biblical wisdom to set us straight. What we need is the Great Physician to heal our overscheduled souls.

If only we could make time for an appointment.

3

The Killer P's

Diagnosis #1: You Are Beset with
Many Manifestations of Pride

I suppose every writer has different routines for writing. When I know what my next book is going to be, I start reading for it about a year in advance. I collect articles and blog posts. I jot down stray thoughts. I usually read twenty to twenty-five books before beginning to write. In preparation for this book I read up on leadership, time management, technology, and Sabbath. Some books were Christian and some weren't. Most were helpful.

But not all. Somehow I stumbled upon a book that initially looked promising, called *Time Warrior*.[1] It must have been well reviewed on Amazon, or maybe it was the endorsement on the back from Jay Adams (different Jay Adams, turns out). For whatever reason, I ordered the book expecting a practical nugget or two on time management. What I found were paragraphs like this one from the preface:

---

[1] Steve Chandler, *Time Warrior: How to Defeat Procrastination, People-Pleasing, Self-Doubt, Over-Commitment, Broken Promises and Chaos* (Anna Maria, FL: Maurice Bassett, 2011).

> This book takes you on a 101-chapter journey intended
> to transmute the base metals of ordinary linear time-
> consciousness into the gold of the Time Warrior's non-lin-
> ear vision. You will learn to create for yourself a newfound
> and more powerful cognitive style that will make time track-
> ing, multi-tasking and other clock-subservient behaviors an
> unsavory and distant memory.[2]

Right. All I have to do is transmute the base metals of time con-
sciousness. It's all coming together. Actually, I'm not sure I understand the essence of a time warrior, other than that he thinks
really positive thoughts, believes in himself, gets going right
now, and does cool things like "dismembers procrastination."[3]

There are plenty of books like *Time Warrior* which promise a revolutionary new approach to the problem of busyness.
After all, who doesn't want to learn long-forgotten secrets
that will change your life forever? And yet, I think we all know
deep down that's not how life works. Transformation is not so
simple. The fixes are not so quick. As Christians, especially, we
ought to know better because we understand deep down that
the problem is not just with our schedules or with the world's
complexity—something is not right *with us*. The chaos is at
least partly self-created. The disorder of daily life is a product
of disorder in the innermost places of the heart. Things are
not the way they ought to be because *we* are not the way we
are supposed to be. Which means our understanding of busyness must start with the one sin that begets so many of our
other sins: pride.

---

[2] Ibid., xi-xii (note: the preface was written by the publisher, Maurice Bassett).
[3] Ibid., 21.

A Meditation on the Many Manifestations of Pride

Pride is subtle and shape-shifting. There is more of it at work in our hearts than we know, and more of it pulsing through our busyness than we realize. Pride is the villain with a thousand faces.

People-pleasing. We are busy because we try to do too many things. We do too many things because we say yes to too many people. We say yes to all these people because we want them to like us and we fear their disapproval. It's not wrong to be kind. In fact, it's the mark of a Christian to be a servant. But people-pleasing is something else. Doing the cookie drive so you can love others is one thing. Doing the cookie drive so that others might love you is quite another. So much of our busyness comes down to meeting people's expectations. You may have a reputation for being the nicest person in the world because the operating principle in your heart is to have a reputation for being the nicest person in the world. Not only is that a manifestation of pride and therefore a sin; it also makes our lives miserable (living and dying by the approval of others), and it usually hurts those who are closest to us (who get what's left over of our time and energy after we try to please everyone else). People often call it low self-esteem, but people-pleasing is actually a form of pride and narcissism.

Pats on the back. This is the most obvious kind of pride: living for praise. It's similar to people-pleasing, except less motivated by fear than by a desire for glory. "If I take on this extra assignment, I'll be a hero to everyone in the office." Never mind what it will mean for my family, my church, or my walk with the Lord, so long as it means more glory for me.

Performance evaluation. As in, we tend to overrate our own. Studies consistently show that almost all students rate themselves above average. Almost all employees consider themselves in the top tier. Almost all pastors think they are strong preachers. Because we regard ourselves so highly, we overestimate our importance. We assume, "If I don't do this, no one will. Everything depends on me." But the truth is, you're only indispensable until you say no. You are unique. Your gifts are important. People love you. But you're not irreplaceable.

After being gone one summer on sabbatical, I came back to hear glowing reviews about how well everything went at the church without me and how marvelously the other pastors preached in my place. Obviously, as the shepherd of the flock, that's just what I wanted to hear. And obviously, as a sinner, it took some getting used to. Part of me would have felt better to hear that everything tanked in my absence.

Possessions. We work to earn, and we earn to spend. We stay busy because we want more stuff. It's not wrong to want a new couch or even a new house. The problem comes when we take pride in our possessions, or, more subtly, when we are too proud to trust in God no matter what happens with our possessions. What does it profit a man to gain the whole world if he has no time to prepare for the world to come?

Proving myself. God is not against ambition. Too many Christians lack the initiative, courage, and diligence that ambition inspires. But ambition for our own glory must not be confused with ambition for God's glory. Some of us never rest because we are still trying to prove something to our parents, our ex-girlfriend, or our high school coach.

Pity. Let's face it: people feel sorry for us when we're busy. If we get our lives under control, we won't seem nearly so impressive and people won't ooh and aah over our burdens. Many of us feel proud to be so busy, and we enjoy the sympathy we receive for enduring such heroic responsibilities.

Poor planning. I can look back and see many times in ministry where I was too hesitant to hand over certain tasks to others. I made my week unbearable and made my family suffer because of being too proud to have someone preach for me or too worried about appearances to have someone lead in my place. I let my planning be dictated by pride rather than by what would best serve my soul, my family, and my church.

Power. "I need to stay busy because I need to stay in control."

Perfectionism. "I can't let up because I can't make a mistake."

Position. "I do too much because that's what people like me are supposed to do."

Prestige. "If I keep pushing myself, I'll finally be somebody. I'll finally matter. I'll finally arrive." Nonsense. You won't be satisfied. The only thing worse than failing to realize any of your dreams, is seeing them all come true. You were meant for something more. Even if you could be known the world over, what does it matter if you have no time to be known by God?

Posting. If we're honest, pride lies behind much of the social media revolution. I've often had to ask myself, "Why am I blogging? Why I am tweeting? Is it for my name and my fame?" It doesn't matter how big or small our following; we can turn Facebook and Twitter into outposts for our glory. Or—and this is more my struggle—we can fear what others will think if we don't show up for hours, days, or weeks. We don't want to disappoint hundreds or thousands of people we've never met, so we work all night and ruin the evening of the few people who depend on us every day.

Here's the bottom line: of all the possible problems contributing to our busyness, it's a pretty good bet that one of the most pervasive is pride.

But What About . . . ?

The easy application at this point is to avoid pride by becoming a boorish, lazy crank. Some people think that if they don't give a rip about the opinions of others and maintain an ambition-less life then they will have conquered pride. But again, real life does not always jibe with our tidy logic. Taming busyness is not as simple as saying no to everything and refusing to please anyone. Real life applications get tricky when we think about them. Consider questions like these:

- If I give up thirty minutes to run an errand at my wife's request, is that people-pleasing or is it being a good husband? What if I do the same for a friend? What about for a complete stranger?
- If I like to meet other people's expectations, does that make me servile—or does it mean I'm a humble servant?
- Should I take into consideration the favors this friend has done for me when considering the favor he wants me to do for him?
- When is it right to sacrifice my comfort, or the comfort of those I love, so that I can keep my word?
- If perfectionism is wrong, should I *not* strive for excellence?
- Are you saying we shouldn't care about community standards or cultural expectations?

- Is the safest course of action, then, to simply do what I want and never consider the thoughts of others?

As you can gather from these questions, pride is not always easy to detect. While we may all, to some degree, be busy because of pride, that doesn't mean every bit of busyness is the direct result of pride. Every one of the P's listed in the previous section could be changed from vice into virtue with just a minor tweak. People-pleasing could be loving your neighbor as yourself. Poor planning could be a willingness to sacrifice for the sake of others. Considering your position could be seen as having a sense of duty to your calling. So how can we tell when we are frantic and overwhelmed because of pride and when we are busy for nobler reasons?

Who Is This For?

I can't answer that question for every person in every situation. God grants wisdom and discernment and good friends to help us understand our hearts. But I can suggest one diagnostic question that has been helpful to me. As I try to discern what's people-pleasing, self-aggrandizing pride, and what's genuine service to others, I try to keep in mind this simple question: *Am I trying to do good or to make myself look good?*

Granted, this doesn't solve all our problems. We can still get overbusy genuinely loving people. And many times we get involved with people or projects for a whole myriad of motivations that we can't fully untangle. My diagnostic question isn't a discernment grid all by itself. But it's a start.

Suppose you are asked to coach your daughter's soccer

team. You don't really want to, and you know your schedule is already packed, but reluctantly you say yes. Good move or bad move? That depends. Maybe you said yes and agreed to inconvenience yourself because you want to spend more time with your daughter and you want to influence the lives of her teammates. But just as likely, you said yes because you didn't want to let people down and you didn't want to disappoint the person making the request. In other words, you gave yourself one more thing to do so that you might look good before others. Ask yourself: Am I serving me or serving them? Saying yes always looks like the latter, but it's often all about the former.

Or think about how you help people who are hurting. We all have needy people in our lives, the kind that never get enough attention and always demand more of our time. Here's what usually happens in situations like this. At first we try to help, maybe even enthusiastically so. But as the demands escalate, we despair of ever being free from this relationship. We begin to resent the person we wanted so much to help. And yet the calls for help keep coming. What's a busy person to do? We could immediately cut off all contact or ignore the person to oblivion. But that only serves our interests. On the flip side, we could continue to be at this friend's beck and call. But that probably doesn't serve our friend's interests either. It makes us look good and feel noble, but it doesn't confront the unhealthy pattern of dependency. In all likelihood, the friend has experienced a parade of people in her life who get exhausted by her demands and fly away. What she really needs, and how you could best serve her, is an honest conversation about what you can and cannot do for her. This is the most difficult approach,

4

The Terror of
Total Obligation

Diagnosis #2: You Are Trying to Do What
God Does Not Expect You to Do

I've already talked about some of the ways I was crazy busy in seminary. But I haven't talked about all the good things I wanted to do but didn't have time for. I had a lot of fun in seminary, with good friends, good books, and more Mario Kart than I ever anticipated. It was a great season of life. But I also felt burdened. Not only by all the things I was doing, but by all the things I *could* have been doing.

High school and college had plenty of opportunities too, but in seminary all of the opportunities were "this-is-what-good-Christians-do" kinds of opportunities. I tried my best, but I didn't go to every chapel. I didn't take advantage of every special speaker. I didn't attend every praise and worship rally or every theological symposium. I didn't take advantage of the events put on by the evangelism committee, and the one time

I did—going down to Salem for street evangelism on Hallow-een—I felt terrible afterward for barely sharing my faith with any of the drunk witches I ran into.

I attended a lot of prayer meetings at seminary, but not half as many as some of my friends. I was passionate about missions in the 10/40 window, but not nearly as passionate as my classmates who had already served there. I knew youth ministry was important, but I wasn't giving my life for at-risk teens as some of my peers were. I just couldn't muster sufficient enthusiasm for all the good causes and inspired ideas right in front of me. I couldn't even keep up with praying for all these good causes. It seemed that I lacked the spiritual wherewithal to do everything necessary for lost people, for the nations, and for God's glory.

Doing More for God

I understand there are lazy people out there who need to get radical for Jesus. I understand that many people are stingy with their resources and fritter their time away on inane television shows. I understand there are lots of Christians in our churches sitting around doing nothing who need to be challenged not to waste their life. I am deeply thankful for preachers and writers who challenge us to risk everything and make our lives count. I know a lot of sleepy Christians in need of a wake-up call.

But I also know people like me, people who easily feel a sense of responsibility, people who easily feel bad for not doing more. I was the kid in grade school who was ready to answer every question the teacher asked. I signed up for things just because they were offered. I took on extra credit just to be safe. I never skipped a class in college and would have felt bad for missing any chapel service. I took the practice ACT the year before I *really* took the practice ACT, which was a year before I took the real ACT. For all sorts of reasons—pride, diligence, personality—opportunities have often felt like obligations to me.

And surely I'm not the only one. Surely there are many Christians who are terribly busy because they sincerely want to be obedient to God. We hear sermons that convict us for not praying more. We read books that convince us to do more for global hunger. We talk to friends who inspire us to give more and read more and witness more. The needs seem so urgent. The workers seem so few. If we don't do something, who will? We want to be involved. We want to make a difference. We want to do what's expected of us. But there just doesn't seem to be the time.

Thing One and Thing Two
(and Thing Three and Thing Four . . .)

The Bible is a big book, and there's a lot in there. So the Bible says a lot about the poor, about marriage, about prayer, about evangelism, about missions, about justice; it says a lot about a lot. Almost any Christian can make a case that their thing should be the main thing or at least one of the most important things. It's easy for preachers and leaders, or just plain old Christian friends, to pound away at "more"—we should pray more, give more, show hospitality more, share our faith more, read our Bibles more, volunteer more. Maybe it's because I'm type A or left-brained or a beaver or an ESTJ or a good pastor or a people-pleasing sinner, but I feel these "more" imperatives poignantly. That's why the "do not" commands are like a breath of fresh air. "Do not commit murder"—that's tough if you take the heart level seriously (see Matt. 5:21–26). But I don't have to put the sixth commandment on my to-do list. It doesn't require me to start a nonprofit or spend another evening away from my family. I just (just!) need to put to death the deeds of the flesh, die to myself, and live to Christ.

Not killing someone or not committing adultery or not taking the Lord's name in vain are not easy commands. But they don't overwhelm me. Doing something about the global AIDS crisis, tackling homelessness, getting water to an impoverished village—these overwhelm me. Along with some of the advice I've gotten about pastoral ministry: make sure you do a few hours of counseling a week; make sure you are working to develop leaders every week; make sure you are doing one-on-one discipleship every week; make sure you do a few hours of evangelism every week; make sure you reserve half a day for reading every week; make sure you are spending time in Greek and Hebrew every week. Who is sufficient for these things?

And that's to say nothing about humanitarian crises and community service. I know the Bible says a lot about "widows and orphans." But what do I *do*? Where do I start? Where do I find the time? How can I possibly meet all these obligations? I have five children and a full-time job. I try to be generous with my money, try to share my faith once in awhile, try to do family devotions more often than not, try to take my wife out on a date every other week, try to respond to needs in my church, and try to pray for the poor and the lost. Is it possible that God is not asking me to do anything about sex trafficking right now?

Calming the Crazy Man Inside

Before you think I'm a total nut-job and scream, "Physician, heal thyself!" let me hasten to add: I do understand the gospel. I know that all this talk of what I should be doing or could be doing is not healthy. I know that. And I'm really doing fine. I'm not on the verge of burnout or breakdown. I don't feel pressure to keep the earth spinning on its axis. Most days I don't feel guilty about all the stuff I'm not doing.

But getting to the place where my conscience can rest has been a process. I think most Christians hear these urgent calls to do more (or feel them internally already) and learn to live with a low-level guilt that comes from not doing enough. We know we can always pray more and give more and evangelize more, so we get used to living in a state of mild disappointment with ourselves. That's not how the apostle Paul lived (1 Cor. 4:4), and it's not how God wants us to live, either (Rom. 12:1–2).[1] Either we are guilty of sin—like greed, selfishness, idolatry—and we need to repent, be forgiven, and change. Or something else is going on. It's taken me several years, a lot of reflection, and a bunch of unnecessary busyness to understand that when it comes to good causes and good deeds, "do more or disobey" is not the best thing we can say.

---

[1] See my chapter "The Pleasure of God and the Possibility of Godliness," in *The Hole in Our Holiness* (Wheaton, IL: Crossway, 2012).

Here are some of thoughts that have helped me get out from under the terror of total obligation.

I am not the Christ. The senior sermon for my graduating class at seminary was given by Gordon Hugenberger of Park Street Church in Boston. The sermon was based on John the Baptist's words, "I freely confess I am not the Christ." Hugenberger's point to a group of soon-to-be pastors was simple: "You may be part of the bridal party, but you are not the groom. You are not the Messiah, so don't try to be. Along with the Apostles' Creed and the Belgic Confession and the Westminster Confession, make sure you confess John the Baptist's creed: I am not the Christ." I still have a copy of the sermon and listen to it whenever I can find a tape deck. Our Messianic sense of obligation would be greatly relieved if we confessed more regularly what we are not.

There is good news. I was also helped with my busyness issues in seminary by reading a little book by Tim Dearborn called *Beyond Duty: A Passion for Christ, a Heart for Mission.*[2] Dearborn, the director of faith and development for World Vision, argues that for too long the church has motivated people to mission by news of natural catastrophes, complex humanitarian disasters, unreached people groups, and oppressed and exploited minorities. We've been given statistics and stories about the all-too-sad conditions of the world. The good news of Christ's death and resurrection, Dearborn maintains, has been turned into bad news about all the problems in the world and how much more we have to do to make things right. The

---

[2] Tim Dearborn, *Beyond Duty: A Passion for Christ, a Heart for Mission* (Federal Way, WA: World Vision, 1997).

take-home then becomes: serve more, give more, care more, do more. Dearborn reminds us that the gospel is good news of great joy, and that God is the only hope for the world.

Care is not the same as do. At the Lausanne missions gathering in 2010, John Piper made the statement that "we should care about all suffering, especially eternal suffering." He chose the word "care" quite carefully. He didn't want to say we should *do* something about all suffering, because we can't do something about everything. But we can care. This means when we hear about grinding poverty or legal abortion or biblical illiteracy, we are not indifferent. We think and feel that these things ought not to be so. We won't all care about every issue in the same way, but there are some issues we should all care about, some issues that should at least prick our hearts and prompt us to pray. Not giving a rip about sex slaves is not an option for the Christian. Not doing something *directly* to combat this particular evil *is* an option.

We have different gifts and different callings. Every Christian must be prepared to give an answer for the reason for the hope that we have (1 Pet. 3:15), but not everyone will do beach evangelism. Every Christian should be involved in the Great Commission, but not everyone will move overseas. Every Christian should oppose abortion, but not everyone will adopt or volunteer at a crisis pregnancy center. We need Christians who spend their lives improving inner-city schools and Christians whose dream is to get great theological books translated into Polish. And we need Christians who don't make others feel guilty (and don't feel guilty themselves) when one of us follows a different passion than another. I read and write a lot. That's what I do well. But that doesn't mean anyone should feel guilty for not reading and writing as much as I do. You have your own gifts and calling. We have to be okay with other Christians doing certain good things better and more often than we do.

Remember the church. The only work that absolutely must be done in the world is Christ's work. And Christ's work is accomplished through Christ's body. The church—gathered in worship on Sunday and scattered through its members throughout the week—is able to do exponentially more than any of us alone. I can respond to Christ's call in one or two ways, but I am a part of an organism and organization that can respond and serve in a million ways.

I can always pray right now. Prayer can feel like the biggest burden of all. We can always pray more, and we can't possibly pray for every need in the world. Even if we are extremely organized and disciplined, we won't be able to consistently pray for more than a handful of people and problems. But that doesn't mean our prayers are limited to the items we can write on a 3 × 5 card. If your aunt's cousin has upcoming heart surgery, pray immediately after you hear about it. When a missionary shares her requests, pray right on the spot for them. Don't let the moment pass you by. Pray a short prayer. Trust God for the results and, in many cases, move on.

Jesus didn't do it all. Jesus didn't meet every need. He left people waiting in line to be healed. He left one town to preach to another. He hid away to pray. He got tired. He never interacted with the vast majority of people on the planet. He spent thirty years in training and only three years in ministry. He did not try to do it all. And yet, he did everything God asked him to do.

Take Time to Be Holy

I pray that nothing in this chapter encourages you to embrace cheap grace or easy believism. We all have a cross to carry. But it's a cross that kills our sins, smashes our idols, and teaches us the folly of self-reliance. It's a cross that says I'll do anything to *follow* Jesus, not a cross that says I have to do everything *for* Jesus.

No doubt some Christians need to be shaken out of their lethargy and to get busy for the kingdom. But many Christians are too busy already. I can take "redeem the time" (see Eph. 5:16, KJV) as a summons to better time management when in reality it's a call to be holy more than a call to possess the seven habits of highly effective people. I can turn every "is" into an "ought." I can overlook the role that necessity and proximity play in establishing divine obligations.[3] I can forget that my circle of influence will inevitably be smaller than my circle of concern.

Above all, I can lose sight of the good news that the universe is not upheld by the word of *my* power (see Heb. 1:3). That's Christ's work, and no one else can do it. Hallelujah—he doesn't even expect me to try.

---

[3] Cf. Kevin DeYoung and Greg Gilbert, *What Is the Mission of the Church: Making Sense of Social Justice, Shalom, and the Great Commission* (Wheaton, IL: Crossway, 2011), 183–186, 225. See also my article "Stewardship, Obligation, and the Poor," at http://www.9marks.org/journal/obligation-stewardship-and-poor.

5

Mission Creep

Diagnosis #3: You Can't Serve Others
without Setting Priorities

For years this passage from Mark has boggled my mind:

> And rising very early in the morning, while it was still dark,
> he departed and went out to a desolate place, and there he
> prayed. And Simon and those who were with him searched
> for him, and they found him and said to him, "Everyone
> is looking for you." And he said to them, "Let us go on
> to the next towns, that I may preach there also, for that
> is why I came out." And he went throughout all Galilee,
> preaching in their synagogues and casting out demons.
> (Mark 1:35–39)

We think of this passage as a call to prayer. And it is. But
just as much it's a remarkable statement of how resolutely the
Son of Man stayed on mission. Jesus amazes me. His incarnation, his resurrection, his ascension, his exaltation—these defy
description. But I'm also amazed by the more mundane things
about his life, like the fact that he never uttered a thoughtless

word, never spent a wasted day, never strayed from his Father's plan. I have often marveled to think that Jesus was so terrifically busy, but only with the things he was supposed to be doing.

Many of us are so familiar with the Gospels that we fail to see the obvious: Jesus was a very busy man. One of Mark's favorite words is "immediately." For three years, Jesus and his band of disciples are a whirlwind of activity. One event immediately follows another. In Mark 1, Jesus begins his public ministry by teaching in the synagogue, rebuking an unclean spirit, caring for Simon's mother-in-law, and then staying up late into the night, healing many who were sick with various diseases and casting out many demons (1:34). At one point Jesus was too busy to even eat, and his family thought he was going nuts (3:20–21). Jesus had crowds coming to him all the time. He had people looking for him, demanding his time and attention. The impression we get from the Gospels is that almost every day for three years he's preaching, healing, and casting out demons. Don't think Jesus is some kind of Zen master who does yoga and ponders the sound of one hand clapping. If Jesus were alive today, he'd get more e-mails than any of us. He'd have people calling his cell all the time. He'd have a zillion requests for interviews, television appearances, and conference gigs. Jesus did not float above the fray, untouched by the pressures of normal human existence. Our Lord did not sit around listening to harp music all day while the angels brought him heavenly bananas. Jesus was tempted in every way just as we are, yet without sin (Heb. 4:15). And that includes the temptation to be sinfully busy.

But he wasn't. Sinful, that is. He was busy, but never in a

way that made him frantic, anxious, irritable, proud, envious, or distracted by lesser things. When all Capernaum waited for his healing touch, he left for a desolate place to pray. And when the disciples told him to get back to work, he left for another town to preach. Jesus knew the difference between urgent and important. He understood that all the good things he *could* do were not necessarily the things he *ought* to do.

Jesus's Mission and Ours

It's easy to assume that Jesus had fewer pressures on his time than we do. You may think to yourself, "Look, it's nice that Jesus could sneak away in the morning to pray, but he didn't have to get the kids' breakfast. He didn't have to be at work by seven o'clock. He didn't have deadlines and e-mails and business meetings and clients to keep happy." And that's all true. But Jesus didn't have an office he could go to and close the door. Jesus didn't have lunch breaks by himself. Jesus didn't have a house or an apartment or even a room to call his own. He had disciples following him. He had crowds clamoring for him. He had so many people after his time and attention that he was known to jump into boats just to get away.

Don't think Jesus can't sympathize with your busyness. You have bills that need to be paid? Jesus had lepers who wanted to be healed. You have kids screaming for you? Jesus had demons calling him by name. You have stress in your life? Jesus taught large crowds all over Judea and Galilee with people constantly trying to touch him, trick him, and kill him. He had every reason to be run over by a hundred expectations and a thousand great opportunities.

And yet, he stayed on mission. Jesus knew his priorities and stuck with them. Isn't this astounding? Think about it: Jesus wasn't just turning down an opportunity to play in the community soccer league. He said no to people who had diseases—diseases he could have healed instantly. The disciples didn't understand why he wasn't attending to the urgent needs right in front of him. You can hear the note of reproach in their voices: "Everyone is looking for you" (Mark 1:37). In other words, "What are you doing? There's work to do. You're a smashing success. People are lined up waiting for you to help them. Come on! The crowd is getting restless. We're all waiting for you." And Jesus says, "Let's go somewhere else." That amazes me.

Jesus understood his mission. He was not driven by the needs of others, though he often stopped to help hurting people. He was not driven by the approval of others, though he cared deeply for the lost and the broken. Ultimately, Jesus was driven by the Spirit. He was driven by his God-given mission. He knew his priorities and did not let the many temptations of a busy life deter him from his task. For Jesus that meant itinerant preaching, with devoted times of prayer, on his way to the cross.

What are your priorities? What's your mission? More than ten years ago I scrawled down on a yellow legal pad three priorities for my life:

1. To faithfully preach the Word of God.
2. To love and lead my family.
3. To be happy and holy in Jesus Christ.

Obviously, just writing these down has not solved my problem with busyness, but knowing what my life is about has helped me recalibrate my schedule whenever I come to my senses. It's not terribly important that you write out your priorities in a few pithy statements. Some of our priorities may change over time. I'm not giving you one more thing to do. What's important, however, is to think about what really *ought* to matter compared to what really *is* mattering.

For many of us, our de facto mission is:

1. Take care of the house.
2. Meet the next deadline.
3. Keep the people in my life relatively happy.

We would never say those are our priorities, but when it comes to making decisions and managing our time, these become our operative principles. Without forethought of purpose and follow-through of plan, we will keep pushing aside the priorities we *say* are our actual priorities, the important things like God, church, family, and friends. If Jesus had to be deliberate with his priorities, so will we. We will have to work hard to rest. We will have to be dedicated to being disciplined. We will have to make it our mission to stay on mission.

And this means coming to grips with three unassailable truths.

Truth #1: I Must Set Priorities because I Can't Do It All

The person who never sets priorities is the person who does not believe in his own finitude. We don't expect to be able to buy anything we want, because we know there is a limit to our money. But somehow we live as if time knew no bounds, when in fact time is much more limited than money. Wealth can be created, but no one has the ability to grow more time. As Peter Drucker observes, "The supply of time is totally inelastic. No matter how high the demand, the supply will not go up. There is no price for it and no marginal utility curve for it. Moreover, time is totally perishable and cannot be stored. Yesterday's time is gone forever and will never come back. Time is, therefore, always in exceedingly short supply."[1] Time may be our scarcest and most precious resource. And we will begin to use it well only when we realize we do not have an infinite supply to use.

One of the most talked about essays from the past few years was entitled "Why Women Still Can't Have It All," by Anne-Marie Slaughter.[2] Ms. Slaughter was working for Hillary Clinton at the State Department as the first woman director of policy planning when she realized she could not be both the professional and the parent she wanted to be. She knew she had to make a choice, and it was a choice women seem hardwired to make more than men:

> Here I step onto treacherous ground, mined with stereotypes. From years of conversation and observations, however, I've come to believe that men and women respond quite differently when problems at home force them to recognize that their absence is hurting a child, or at least that

---

[1] Peter Drucker, *The Effective Executive: The Definitive Guide to Getting the Right Things Done* (New York: Harper Business, 2006), 26.

[2] Anne-Marie Slaughter, "Why Women Still Can't Have It All," *The Atlantic*, July/August 2012.

their presence would likely help. I do not believe fathers love their children any less than mothers do, but men do seem more likely to choose their job at a cost to their family, while women seem more likely to choose their family at a cost to their job.

Slaughter's sentiments echo those of Mary Matalin when she left her position in the Bush administration: "I finally asked myself, 'Who needs me more?' And that's when I realized, it's somebody else's turn to do this job. I'm indispensable to my kids, but I'm not close to indispensable to the White House."[3] Both of these high-powered women, from different sides of the political aisle, concluded that no matter how much you try to lay out your future or how supportive your husband might be, you still can't have it all.[4] In the real world of finite time, we often have to discern good and better from best.

We'd like to think we are unique, that we can do two (or three or four) things at once better than normal people. But very likely we can't. In his book *The Myth of Multitasking*, Dave Crenshaw argues that the brain really can't put forth effort in two mental processes at the same time.[5] We can do two things at once when one does not require mental effort. We can walk and have a conversation at the same time. We can eat potato chips and watch TV at the same time. But you can't e-mail

---

[3] Quoted in ibid.
[4] Slaughter argues that it's not possible for a woman to have it all even if she plans to have some now (like her career) and some later (like her family). There are simply not enough years for most women to excel at parenting and then climb to the top of a profession (or vice versa). On top of that, Slaughter admits, "I lived that nightmare: for three years, beginning at age 35, I did everything possible to conceive and was frantic at the thought that I had simply left having a biological child until it was too late."
[5] Dave Crenshaw, *The Myth of Multitasking: How "Doing It All" Gets Nothing Done* (San Francisco: Jossey-Bass, 2008), 29–33.

and talk on the phone at the same time, or finish a report and talk to your son at the same time. We may think we are multi-tasking, but we are actually "switch-tasking." This is true of computers too. They give the appearance of multitasking, but in reality they are switching back and forth between various programs at rapid speed. If computers can't do two things at once, we certainly can't.

Setting priorities can be difficult. Sticking to them can seem impossible. But Jesus understands the challenge. He lived with unrelenting demands and unbelievable pressure. He also knew that if he were to accomplish the purposes God had for him, he would have to pass up ten thousand good purposes other people had for his life. The Son of God could not meet all the needs around him. He had to get away to pray. He had to eat. He had to sleep. He had to say no. If Jesus had to live with human limitations, we'd be foolish to think we don't. The people on this planet who end up doing nothing are those who never realized they couldn't do everything.

Truth #2: I Must Set Priorities If I Am to Serve Others Most Effectively

I once heard a conference speaker tell the story about a certain "Jane" who came to him for counseling. Jane arrived for her first counseling appointment forty-five minutes late and in a fluster. After promising to do better, she arrived just as late the second time. And the third time. And on and on. Jane didn't mean to be late, just as she didn't mean for her whole life to feel like an undisciplined failure. She had every intention of being on time and even planned carefully to do so. But something would always come up. She'd stop to pray for someone or pull over to run an errand or say yes to a new request. Jane lived a priority-less life. Whatever was right in front of her became her new number-one priority. The speaker called her a wonderful woman you'd never want to hire.

We shouldn't be too hard on Jane. In some ways, she's exactly what a Christian should be. She is willing to do anything for anyone at any time. Maybe Jane would be the most popular woman in her village in some other country. But, no matter the culture, there is something not quite right about Jane's decision making. Her weakness is that by trying to meet the needs right in front of her, she's unable to keep the commitments she's already made. It may be understandable the first time she leaves her family waiting for an hour in order to catch up with an old friend. But if it happens again and again, we'd wonder how well she is serving those who need her the most.

It's taken me a while to see this, but now I do. And I absolutely believe it: I can't serve others effectively without setting priorities. If I respond to every e-mail, show up at every possible meeting, and have coffee with every person asking for "just a few minutes," I won't have time to adequately prepare for my sermon. I may help several people during the week, but I won't faithfully serve the many more who come on Sunday. If I attend every possible church function, I won't be there for my son's basketball game. Stewarding my time is not about selfishly pursuing only the things I like to do. It's about effectively serving others in the ways I'm best able to serve and in the ways I am most uniquely called to serve.

This means, in addition to setting priorities, I must

establish *posteriorities*. This is Drucker's word for the things that should be at the end (posterior) of our to-do list. These are the things we decide *not* to do for the sake of doing the things we ought to do. Making goals is not enough. We must establish what tasks and troubles we will not tackle at all.[6] Several years ago my elders made a rule that I couldn't do any more premarital counseling. They didn't fear for my own marriage. They weren't trying to "protect" me from interacting with people. I still am very involved in day-to-day pastoral ministry. They had simply concluded, with my input, that this was not the best use of my time. In order to have time for my priorities, they made this activity a posteriority for me.

One reason we never tame the busyness beast is because we are unwilling to kill anything. We rearrange our schedule and tighten up our breaks, but nothing improves because we haven't pruned anything. We haven't established what we won't do any longer. Setting priorities is an expression of love for others and for God. "Unseized" time tends to flow toward our weakness, get swallowed up by dominant people, and surrender to the demands of emergencies.[7] So unless God intends for us to serve only the loudest, neediest, most intimidating people, we need to plan ahead, set priorities, and serve more wisely so that we might serve more effectively.

And notice, the word is *effective*, not *efficient*. Caring for people is often wildly inefficient. People are messy, and if we are going to help them we will wade into a lot of time-

---

[6] Drucker, *Effective Executive*, 110–111.

[7] These three items come from Gordon MacDonald, *Ordering Your Private World* (Nashville: Oliver Nelson, 1985), 74–79. MacDonald also includes a fourth item: unseized time gets invested in things that gain public acclamation.

consuming messes. God doesn't expect his servants to all be type A, detail-oriented, Excel spreadsheet gurus. Efficiency is not the goal. But if Jesus is any example, God does expect us to say no to a whole lot of good things so that we can be freed up to say yes to the most important things he has for us.

Truth #3: I Must Allow Others to Set Their Own Priorities

Last year, while sharing dinner with other speakers at a conference, I was able to sit next to one of my favorite Christian musicians. Being a big fan for many years, I was excited to finally meet the man, who proved to be as kind and thoughtful as I'd hoped. In the course of conversation I learned that this man had a family connection in East Lansing. So naturally, I quickly suggested that we should get together sometime when he was in town. He seemed amenable to the idea. So I pressed a little further and asked if he wanted to lead worship for us some Sunday when he was in the area. The man quickly and graciously demurred, explaining that he needed to be at his church on weekends and couldn't lead worship in other churches.

I was not at all offended by his response. In fact, I respected him for letting me know it wouldn't work. My own tendency is to be overly accommodating when put on the spot by an invitation like that. I usually overcommit and lead people on, rather than stating up front what my priorities are (probably because I like pats on the back and prestige and so many of the other P's in chapter 3). I was thankful that this accomplished musician knew his priorities and was not going to change them on a whim just because some new acquaintance asked him to.

Like most other problems in the Christian life, battling

busyness is a community project. It's not enough to set priorities ourselves, if we don't respect that others must set them too. Here's where we can help each other immensely. Don't always expect the lunch request to work. Don't get upset when your "what do you think?" e-mail doesn't get answered. Don't be offended if your need doesn't go to the top of the pile. Understand that people often say "I'm busy" because saying "I have many priorities in life and right now you aren't one of them" would be too painful. Don't think it rude if some people have less availability for you than you have for them. And don't begrudge people the time you are so desperately fighting for. Unless we're God, none of us deserve to be the priority for everyone else all the time.

6

A Cruel Kindergarchy

Diagnosis #4: You Need to Stop
Freaking Out about Your Kids

There is almost no way for parents to completely remove busyness from their lives. Children don't afford that luxury. But with a little effort—and a lot of lightening up—most of us can be a little less busy and a lot less crazy.

We live in a strange new world. Kids are safer than ever before, but parental anxiety is skyrocketing. Children have more options and more opportunities, but parents have more worry and hassle. We have put unheard-of amounts of energy, time, and focus into our children. And yet, we assume their failures will almost certainly be our fault for not doing enough. We live in an age where the future happiness and success of our children trumps all other concerns. No labor is too demanding, no expense is too high, and no sacrifice is too great for our children. A little life hangs in the balance, and everything depends on us.

You might call this child-obsessed parenting an expression of sacrificial love and devotion. And it might be. But you could also call it Kindergarchy: rule by children. "Under Kindergarchy," Joseph Epstein observes, "all arrangements are centered on children: their schooling, their lessons, their predilections, their care and feeding and general high maintenance—children are the name of the game."[1] Parents become little more than indentured servants attending to their children as if they were direct descendants of the Sun King. "Every child a dauphin" is how Epstein puts it.

Becoming a stern, exacting disciplinarian is not the antidote to Kindergarchy. Epstein is not pining for parents to be harsher, just less harangued. It's worth remembering that not long ago the nuclear family was much less child-centered. Epstein, now in his sixties, recalls never being unhappy as a kid. And yet, his experience as a child would be considered almost criminal today:

> My mother never read to me, and my father took me to no ballgames, though we did go to Golden Gloves fights a few times. When I began my modest athletic career, my parents never came to any of my games, and I should have been embarrassed had they done so. My parents never met any of my girlfriends in high school. No photographic or video record exists of my uneven progress through early life. My father never explained about the birds and the bees to me; his entire advice on sex, as I clearly remember, was, "You want to be careful."[2]

Granted, Epstein is not a Christian and did not grow up as a Christian. I'm not holding up his childhood as a model for us

---

[1] Joseph Epstein, "The Kindergarchy: Every Child a Dauphin," *The Weekly Standard* 13/37 (June 9, 2008).
[2] Ibid.

all. Neither is he. His experience is not as important as the fact that his experience was not at all unusual. What's important is the realization—one any of our parents could confirm—that today's family is structured around the life of the child as never before. Man has not always lived under Kindergarchy.

The Myth of the Perfect Parent

Parenting has become more complicated than it needs to be. It used to be, as far as I can tell, that Christian parents basically tried to feed their kids, clothe them, teach them about Jesus, and keep them away from explosives. Now our kids have to sleep on their backs (no, wait, their tummies; no, never mind, their backs), while listening to Baby Mozart and surrounded by scenes of *Starry, Starry Night*. They have to be in piano lessons before they are five and can't leave the car seat until they're about five foot six.

It's all so involved. There are so many rules and expectations. Parenting may be the last bastion of legalism. Not just in the church, but in our culture. We live in a permissive society that won't count any sin against you as an adult, but will count the calories in your kids' hot lunches. I keep hearing that kids aren't supposed to eat sugar anymore. What a world! What a world! My parents were solid as a rock, but we still had a cupboard populated with cereal royalty like Captain Crunch and Count Chocula. In our house the pebbles were fruity and the charms were lucky. The breakfast bowl was a place for marshmallows, not dried camping fruit. Our milk was 2%. And sometimes, if we needed to take the edge off a rough morning, we'd tempt fate and chug a little vitamin D.

As nanny parents living in a nanny state, we think of our children as amazingly fragile and entirely moldable. Both assumptions are mistaken. It's harder to ruin our kids than we think and harder to stamp them for success than we'd like. Christian parents in particular often operate with an implicit determinism. We fear that a few wrong moves will ruin our children forever, and at the same time assume that the right combination of protection and instruction will invariably produce godly children. Leslie Leyland Fields is right: "One of the most resilient and cherished myths of parenting is that parenting creates the child."[3]

A Debilitating Determinism

Selfish Reasons to Have More Kids is the provocative book by Bryan Caplan, a professor of economics at George Mason University. Here's his thesis: parents make their work more difficult than it has to be because they overestimate how much depends on them for the future well-being of their children. He cites numerous twin and adoption studies which conclude that with almost every desirable trait parents wish to pass on to their children—from health to happiness to intelligence to success to general affability—nature is more influential than nurture. For decades, researchers in multiple studies have followed the lives of biological twins who have grown up in different families. While upbringing can make a big difference in the short run, scholars argue that, in the long run, grown twins display

---

[3] Leslie Leyland Fields, "The Myth of the Perfect Parent: Why the Best Parenting Techniques Don't Produce Christian Children," *Christianity Today*, January 2010.

than they need to be. While we can't avoid being busy with our children—indeed, it's a biblical command (Titus 2:5)—with a good dose of prayer, a shot of biblical reflection, and a little common sense, we can avoid freaking out about them quite so much.

personality and sociological behaviors owing more to heredity than to environment.

Caplan emphasizes—and this is extremely important—that these studies focus on middle-class families in First World countries. Families that get approved for adoption tend to be healthy, loving, and stable. Caplan is not suggesting that parents make no difference whatsoever. In fact, he advocates international adoption as one way of making a huge difference in a child's life. His contention, though, is that within the framework of a pretty "normal" family in the developed world, different approaches to parenting do little to determine the kind of adult the child will become.

Interestingly, Caplan mentions three traits that are more susceptible to parental influence. The first two are politics and religion. To be fair, Caplan is quick to claim that these variations are superficial, that in the end nurture doesn't matter all that much for a person's *deeper* political and religious orientation.[4] But even if heart-level commitment in these areas could be measured—and I'm not sure it can be—these two exceptions are still significant. Different family environments didn't have much effect on the twins' grades, health, or success, but they did have a big effect on religious and political affiliation.[5]

The other trait particularly influenced by upbringing is appreciation. The twin and adoption studies show that "parents have a noticeable effect on how kids experience and remember their childhood."[6] How we parent matters less than we think

---

[4] Bryan D. Caplan, *Selfish Reasons to Have More Kids* (New York: Basic Books, 2011), 165.
[5] Ibid., 62–65.
[6] Ibid., 88.

when it comes to the sort of person our kids will become in twenty years, but it still matters a great deal in determining what our kids' present experience will be and how they will remember their childhood twenty years from now. We may not be able to shape our child's future identity as much as we'd like, but we can profoundly shape their experience of childhood in the present.

That's why one of the best things we can do for our kids is to find a way to stop being so frantic and frazzled. In the "Ask the Children" survey, researcher Ellen Galinsky interviewed more than a thousand children in grades three through twelve and asked parents to guess how kids would respond. One key question asked the kids what one thing they would change about the way their parents' work was affecting them. The results were striking. The kids rarely wished for more time with their parents, but, much to the parents' surprise, they wished their parents were less tired and less stressed.

Similarly, Galinsky asked kids to grade their parents in a dozen areas. Overall, parents did pretty well, with both moms and dads right around a B. Most parents got an A when it came to making their children feel important and being able to attend important events in their lives. The biggest weakness, according to the kids, was anger management. More than 40 percent of kids gave their moms and dads a C, D, or F on controlling their temper. It was the worst grade on the children's parental report card. Our children, Caplan argues, are suffering from "secondhand stress."[7] By trying to do so much for

---

[7] Ibid., 32–33.

them, we are actually making our kids less happy. It would be better for us and for our kids if we planned fewer outings, got involved in fewer activities, took more breaks from the kids, did whatever we could to get more help around the house, and made parental sanity a higher priority.

My point in unpacking Caplan's book is not to make us all biological determinists. Our genes will never fully explain the variations in human behavior. As Christians, we know that God creates us in his image, as responsible moral agents. DNA does not determine our eternal destiny. But then again, neither does parenting. That's the point. "You can have a better life and a bigger family," Caplan writes, "if you admit that your kids' future is not in your hands."[8]

We must reject our well-meaning but misguided spiritual determinism. As it turns out, it doesn't all depend on us. The Bible is full of examples of spiritual giants producing rascally children and noble kin coming from polluted loins. While the proverbial wisdom of Scripture (Prov. 22:6) and the promises of the covenant (Gen. 17:7) tell us that good Christian parents and good Christian children normally go together, we must concede that God is sovereign (Rom. 9:6–18), salvation is a gift (Eph. 2:8–9), and the wind of the Spirit blows where it wishes (John 3:8). As Fields puts it in her *Christianity Today* article, "Parents with unbelieving children, friends with children in jail, the discoveries of the geneticists, and the faith heroes in Hebrews 11 are all powerful reminders of this truth: We will parent imperfectly, our children will make their own choices,

---

[8] Ibid., 76.

and God will mysteriously and wondrously use it all to advance his kingdom."[9]

Getting a Few Things Right

I sometimes look back at my childhood, think about myself and my three siblings now firmly walking with the Lord, and wonder, "What made my parents so special?" I watched too many *Growing Pains* reruns and played a lot of Super Tecmo Bowl. I never learned to like granola or my vegetables. I don't always chew with my mouth closed. And I can't remember ever getting "the talk" from my dad (unless I have repressed the memory). But I always knew my parents loved me. I'm sure I didn't smile at everything they ever did, but I always wanted to please them.

They made us go to church every Wednesday and twice every Sunday. They made us do our homework. They laid down obvious rules—the kind that keep kids from killing each other. They wouldn't accept any bad language, and I didn't hear any from them. Mom took care of us when we were sick. Dad told us he loved us. I never found porn around the house. My dad read the Bible at the dinner table more often than not. We got in trouble when we broke the rules. And all would be well if we said we were sorry. I don't remember a lot of powerful heart-to-heart conversations. But we knew who we were, where we stood, and what to expect. I'd be thrilled to give my kids the same.

I worry that many young parents are too sure that every decision will set their kids on an unalterable trajectory to

[9] Fields, "Myth of the Perfect Parent."

heaven or hell. It's like my secretary at the church once told me: "Most moms and dads think they are either the best or the worst parents in the world, and both are wrong." Could it be we've made parenting too complicated? Isn't the most important thing not what we do but who we are as parents? They will remember our character before they remember our exact rules regarding television and Twinkies.

I want to grow as a parent—in patience and wisdom and consistency. But I also know that I can't change my kids' hearts. I can't make their decisions for them. I am responsible for my heart and must be responsible to teach my children the way of the Lord. But there's no surefire input—say, the right mix of family devotions, Tolkien, and nutrition—that will infallibly produce the output we desire. Ten years into this parenting gig, I'm just trying to be faithful and to repent for all the times I'm not.

I have five kids and, besides the Lord's grace, I'm banking on the fact that there really are just a few nonnegotiables in raising children. When you think about it, what does the Bible actually say about parenting? Child rearing is hardly the main theme of Scripture. God doesn't provide many specific instructions about the parent-child relationship, except that parents should teach their children about God (Deut. 6:7; Proverbs 1–9), discipline them (Prov. 23:13; Heb. 12:7–11), be thankful for them (Ps. 127:3–5), and not exasperate them (Eph. 6:4). Filling in the details depends on the family, the culture, the Spirit's wisdom, and a whole lot of trial and error.

There are ways to screw up our kids for life, but thankfully the Happy Meal is not one of them. There is not a straight line from Ronald McDonald to eternal rebellion. Much like there is not a direct correlation between doodling loudly in the service as a toddler and doing meth as a teenager. Could it be that, beyond the basics of godly parenting, most of the other techniques and convictions are just nibbling around the edges? Certainly, there are lots of ways that good parents make their kids a little more manageable from day to day, but even the kid hooked on Angry Birds who just downed a pack of Fun Dip and is now watching his fifth Pixar movie of the week still has a decent shot at not being a sociopath.

I remember years ago hearing a line from Alistair Begg, quoting another man, that went like this: "When I was young I had six theories and no kids. Now I have six kids and no theories." I must be ahead of the curve: it took me only five kids to run out of theories.

I could be wrong. My kids are still young. Maybe this no-theory is a theory of its own. I just know that the longer I parent the more I want to focus on doing a few things really well, and not get too worked up about everything else. I want to spend time with my kids, teach them the Bible, take them to church, laugh with them, cry with them, discipline them when they disobey, say "sorry" when I mess up, and pray a ton. I want them to look back and think, "I'm not sure what my parents were doing or if *they* even knew what they were doing. But I always knew my parents loved me, and I knew they loved Jesus."

Maybe our hearts are too busy with fear and worry. Maybe we are overanxious. Maybe we are overcommitted. Maybe we are over-parenting. And maybe we are making our lives crazier

but the one that appropriately reclaims your time while still serving your friend.

Let me give a final example, one that's a little different. Recall the diagnostic question: Am I trying to do them good or trying to look good? Think how this question could sanctify our approach to hospitality.

Opening our home to others is a wonderful gift and a neglected discipline in the church. But we easily forget the whole point of hospitality. Think of it this way: Good *hospital-ity* is making your home a hospital. The idea is that friends and family and the wounded and weary people come to your home and leave helped and refreshed. And yet, too often hospitality is a nerve-wracking experience for hosts and guests alike. Instead of setting our guests at ease, we set them on edge by telling them how bad the food will be, and what a mess the house is, and how sorry we are for the kids' behavior. We get worked up and crazy busy in all the wrong ways because we are more concerned about looking good than with *doing* good. So instead of our encouraging those we host, they feel compelled to encourage us with constant reassurances that everything is just fine. Opening our homes takes time, but it doesn't have to take over our lives. Christian hospitality has much more to do with good relationships than with good food. There is a fine line between care and cumber. In many instances, less ado would serve better.

It's okay to be busy at times. You can't love and serve others without giving of your time. So work hard; work long; work often. Just remember it's not supposed to be about you. Feed people, not your pride.

7

Deep Calls to Deep

Diagnosis #5: You Are Letting the
Screen Strangle Your Soul

The first time I really became aware of the full intensity of
the problem was in a conversation with a couple of students
training for the ministry. I was speaking at one of our top
seminaries when, after the class, two men came up to me in
private to ask a question. I could tell by the way they were
speaking quietly and shifting their eyes that they had something awkward to say. I was sure they were going to talk about
pornography. And sure enough, they wanted to talk about
their struggles with the Internet. But it wasn't porn they were
addicted to. It was social media. They told me they couldn't
stop looking at Facebook, and they were spending hours on
blogs and mindlessly surfing the Web. This was several years
ago, and I didn't know how to help them. I hadn't encountered
this struggle before and wasn't immersed in it myself. Five
years later I have, and I am.

I used to make fun of bloggers. I used to lampoon

Facebook. I used to laugh at Twitter. I've never been an early adopter with technology. I've never cared what Steve Jobs was up to. I used to roll my eyes at technophiles. Until I became one. Now I have a blog, a Facebook page, a Twitter handle, a Bluetooth headset, an iPhone, an iPad, wifi at work and at home, cable TV, a Wii, a Blu-ray player, multiple e-mail accounts, and unlimited texting. Pride comes before a fall.

I was born in 1977, so I can remember life before the digital revolution. In college we had to go to a computer lab to get on the Internet, which wasn't a big deal because nothing happened on e-mail and I didn't see anything interesting online. By the time I was in seminary, however, things had changed. E-mail was a vital way to communicate, and the Internet was how my friends and I were getting our news (and doing fantasy football). But even then (in the late 90s and early 2000s), life was far less connected. I only got an Internet connection in my room partway through seminary—one of those loud, lumbering *ack-ack* dial-up monstrosities. I didn't have a cell phone in high school, college, or graduate school. As little as four or five years ago I didn't do anything on my phone and barely accessed the Internet at home. I'm not suggesting those days were purer and nobler, but my life felt less scattered and less put-upon.

Tech Talk Is Tricky

Writing about technology is fraught with challenges. For starters, some people won't have any idea what I'm talking about. They're probably older and don't understand the attraction

with all these gadgets anyway. The Lord bless you. I hope you enjoy the real world as much as we used to.

Another challenge is that some of the particulars I'm addressing will be out of date in a couple of years, and all of it will sound dated in a few years after that. For example, it's crazy to me that college students hardly do e-mail anymore. You have to text or write them on Facebook if you want their attention.

A third difficulty in writing about technology is the propensity for overreaction. The Luddite impulse is strong among Christians, and it's easy to think the best answer for technology overload is to rage against the machines. And yet, it does no good to pine for a world that isn't coming back and probably wasn't as rosy as we remember it. I like that I can carry the Bible on my phone, and have street maps for the entire country in my pocket, and can check the score whenever I want, and can hear from my friends throughout the day, and can text with my wife while I'm at work. There's no doubt that some things are better because we are all wired to everything.

The problem is that some things aren't better. We must realize that, as the presence of digital devices and digital dependence grows, with this growth comes new capabilities *and* new dangers. The question is not whether the digital revolution adds to the craziness of our lives or whether it poses threats to our souls and our sanity. The question is, what are the threats and what can we do about them?

What Are the Threats?

Much has been written and will be written about the dangers of an insatiable appetite for being plugged in. I'll leave it to others to decide whether Google makes us stupid and whether young people are more or less relational than ever before. Let me simply suggest three ways in which the digital revolution is an accomplice to our experience of being crazy busy. For if we understand the threats, we may have some hope of finding a way forward.

First, there is the threat of addiction. That may sound like too strong a word, but that's what it is. Could you go a whole day without looking at Facebook? Could you go an afternoon without looking at your phone? What about two days away from e-mail? Even if someone promised there would be no emergencies and no new work would come in, we'd still have a hard time staying away from the screen. The truth is, many of us cannot not click. We can't step away, even for a few hours, let alone a few days or weeks.

In his best-selling book *The Shallows*, Nicholas Carr reflects on how his attitude toward the Web has changed. In 2005—the year he says the "Web went 2.0"—he found the digital experience exhilarating. He loved how blogging junked the traditional publishing apparatus. He loved the speed of the Internet, the ease, the hyperlinks, the search engines, the sound, the videos, everything. But then, he recalls, "a serpent of doubt slithered into my infoparadise."[1] He realized that the Net had control over his life in a way that his traditional PC never did. His habits were changing, morphing to accommodate a digital way of life. He became dependent on the

---

[1] Nicholas Carr, *The Shallows: What the Internet Is Doing to Our Brains* (New York: Norton, 2011), 15.

Internet for information and activity. He found his ability to pay attention declining. "At first I'd figured that the problem was a symptom of middle-age mind rot. But my brain, I realized, wasn't just drifting. It was hungry. It was demanding to be fed the way the Net fed it—and the more it was fed, the hungrier it became. Even when I was away from my computer, I yearned to check e-mail, click links, do some Googling. I wanted to be *connected*."[2]

I've noticed the same thing happening to me for the past few years. I can't seem to work for more than fifteen minutes without getting the urge to check my e-mail, glance at a blog, or get caught up on Twitter. It's a terrible feeling. In an afterword to *The Shallows*, Carr explains that after his book came out he heard from dozens of people (usually by e-mail) who wanted to tell their own stories of how the Web had "scattered their attention, parched their memory, or turned them into compulsive nibblers of info-snacks." One college senior sent him a long note describing how he had struggled "with a moderate to major form of Internet addiction" since the third grade. "I am unable to focus on anything in a deep or detailed manner," the student wrote. "The only thing my mind can do, indeed the only thing it wants to do, is plug back into that distracted frenzied blitz of online information." He confessed this, even though he was sure that "the happiest and most fulfilled times of my life have all involved a prolonged separation from the Internet."[3] Many of us are simply overcome—hour after hour, day after day—by the urge to connect online. And

---

[2] Ibid., 16.
[3] Quoted in ibid., 226.

as Christians we know that "whatever overcomes a person, to that he is enslaved" (2 Pet. 2:19).

Second, there is the threat of acedia. Acedia is an old word roughly equivalent to "sloth" or "listlessness." It is not a synonym for leisure, or even laziness. Acedia suggests indifference and spiritual forgetfulness. It's like the dark night of the soul, but more blah, more vanilla, less interesting. As Richard John Neuhaus explains, "Acedia is evenings without number obliterated by television, evenings neither of entertainment nor of education but of narcoticized defense against time and duty. Above all, acedia is apathy, the refusal to engage the pathos of other lives and of God's life with them."[4]

For too many of us, the hustle and bustle of electronic activity is a sad expression of a deeper acedia. We feel busy, but not with a hobby or recreation or play. We are busy with busyness. Rather than figure out what to do with our spare minutes and hours, we are content to swim in the shallows and pass our time with passing the time. How many of us, growing too accustomed to the acedia of our age, feel this strange mix of busyness and lifelessness? We are always engaged with our thumbs, but rarely engaged with our thoughts. We keep downloading information, but rarely get down into the depths of our hearts. That's acedia—purposelessness disguised as constant commotion.

All of this leads directly to the third threat of our digital world, and that's the danger that we are never alone. When I

---

[4] Richard John Neuhaus, *Freedom for Ministry* (Grand Rapids, MI: Eerdmans, 1979), 227.

say "never alone," I'm not talking about Big Brother watching over us or the threat of security breaches. I'm talking about *our desire* to never be alone. Peter Kreeft is right: "We *want* to complexify our lives. We don't have to, we *want* to. We want to be harried and hassled and busy. Unconsciously, we want the very things we complain about. For if we had leisure, we would look at ourselves and listen to our hearts and see the great gaping hole in our hearts and be terrified, because that hole is so big that nothing but God can fill it."[5]

Sometimes I wonder if I'm so busy because I've come to believe the lie that busyness is the point. And nothing allows you to be busy—all the time, with anyone anywhere—like having the whole world in a little black rectangle in your pocket. In *Hamlet's Blackberry*, William Powers likens our digital age to a gigantic room. In the room are more than a billion people. But despite its size, everyone is in close proximity to everyone else. At any moment someone may come up and tap you on the shoulder—a text, a hit, a comment, a tweet, a post, a message, a new thread. Some people come up to talk business, others to complain, others to tell secrets, others to flirt, others to sell you things, others to give you information, others just to tell you what they're thinking or doing. This goes on day and night. Powers calls it a "non-stop festival of human interaction."[6]

We enjoy the room immensely—for awhile. But eventually we grow tired of the constant noise. We struggle to find a

[5] Peter Kreeft, *Christianity for Modern Pagans: Pascal's Pensées Edited, Outlined, and Explained* (San Francisco: Ignatius Press, 1993), 168.
[6] William Powers, *Hamlet's Blackberry: A Practical Philosophy for Building a Good Life in the Digital Age* (New York: Harper, 2010), xii.

personal zone. Someone taps us while we're eating, while we're sleeping, while we're on a date. We even get tapped in the bathroom, for crying out loud. So we decide to take a vacation, just a short one. But no one else seems to know where the exit is. No one else seems interested in leaving. In fact, they all seem put off that you might not want to stay. And even when you find the exit and see the enchanting world through the opening, you aren't sure what life will be like on the other side. It's a leap of faith to jump out and see what happens.

The point of Powers's parable should be self-evident. Like Tolkien's ring, we love the room and hate the room. We want to breathe the undistracted air of digital independence, but increasingly the room is all we know. How can we walk out, when everyone else is staying in? How will we pass our time and occupy our thoughts without the unceasing *tap, tap, tap*? For many of us, the Web is like the Eagles' Hotel California: we can check out anytime we like, but we can never leave.

And the scariest part is that we may not *want* to leave. What if we prefer endless noise to the deafening sound of silence? What if we do not care to hear God's still, small voice? What if the trivialities and distractions of our day are not forced upon us by busyness, or not forced upon us at all? What if we choose to be busy so that we can continue to live with trivia and distraction? If "digital busyness is the enemy of depth,"[7] then we are bound to be stuck in the shallows so long as we're never alone. Our digital age gives new relevance to Pascal's famous line: "I have often said that the sole cause

---

[7] Ibid., 17.

of man's unhappiness is that he does not know how to stay quietly in his room."[8]

Or stay out of the room, as the case may be.

What Can We Do?

So now what? If this is the world we live in and these are the dangers, what's our response? What can we do? Let me offer several ideas, some mainly practical and some more explicitly theological.

Cultivate a healthy suspicion toward technology and "progress." I've already said that technology improves our lives in many ways, so I'm not suggesting we renounce anything with an on/off switch (though that would make your flight attendants happy). But we could do with a little more "distance" from technology, a little more awareness that there was life before the latest innovations and there can be life without it. Neil Postman's admonition is wise: technology "must never be accepted as part of the natural order of things." We must understand that "every technology—from an IQ test to an automobile to a television set to a computer—is a product of a particular economic and political context and carries with it a program, an agenda, and a philosophy that may or may not be life-enhancing and that therefore requires scrutiny, criticism, and control."[9]

Be more thoughtful and understanding in your connectedness with others. Not long ago I noticed a friend of mine, after

---

[8] Blaise Pascal, *Pensées*, trans. A. J. Krailsheimer (New York: Penguin, 1966, rev. ed. 1995), 37.
[9] Neil Postman, *Technopoly: The Surrender of Culture to Technology* (New York: Vintage, 1993), 184–185.

incredibly terse e-mails, was linking to an "e-mail charter" at the end of his messages. I ignored it for weeks (too busy!) but eventually curiosity got the best of me and I clicked on the link. To my surprise the "charter" had very helpful advice about reducing time spent on e-mail: don't ask open-ended questions; don't send back contentless replies; don't cc for no good reason; don't expect an immediate response. It's amazing the way my impatience works. If I text someone, I expect a response in seconds. If I e-mail, I might allow for a couple of hours, but with friends I expect to hear back in a matter of minutes. Cutting back on busyness is a community project. We must allow that slow replies and short replies are not rude. Don't expect with every tap that the other person has to turn his head.

Deliberately use "old" technology. If you don't want to be dependent on your digital devices, make an effort to get by without them. Read a real book. Write a paper letter. Buy a nice pen. Call someone on the phone. Look something up in the dictionary. Drive with the radio off and the iPod unplugged. Go on a run without music. Stop at a bricks-and-mortar store. The goal is not to be quaint, but to relearn a few practices that can be more enjoyable the "old-fashioned" way.

Make boundaries, and fight with all your might to protect them. The simplest step to breaking the tyranny of the screen is also the hardest step: we can't be connected all the time. We have to stop taking our phones to bed. We can't check Facebook during church. We can't text at every meal. Last year my wife and I had one of our biggest fights because she sharply rebuked me for tweeting at the dinner table. She was right to be sharp, and I promised her I would never tweet during dinner again (a promise I think I've kept).

Most families could use a big basket where all the phones and tablets and laptops go to rest for certain hours of every day (dinnertime? devotional time? bedtime? when Dad gets home?). Most of us are long overdue for screen Sabbaths—segments of the day (even whole days) where we will not be "on the grid" or in front of an electronic device. And most of us would find new freedom if we didn't check our phones as the last and first thing we do every day. Of all the little bad habits I have that contribute to my busyness, the habit of checking my e-mail right before I go to bed and checking it as soon as I wake up is probably the worst.

Bring our Christian theology to bear on these dangers of the digital age. While commonsense suggestions are always welcome, our deepest problems can be helped only with the deepest truths. Because of the doctrine of creation, we must affirm that man-made artifacts can be instruments for human flourishing and for the glory of God. So we do not dismiss new technologies out of hand. But because we have a God who chose us in eternity past and looks at a day as a thousand years and a thousand years as a day, we will not be infatuated with the latest fads and trends. And because of the incarnation, we understand there is no substitute for dwelling with physical people in a physical place. So we do not accept virtual encounters as adequate substitutes for flesh and blood relationships.

Likewise, because we understand our worth as image-bearers and our identity as children of God, we will not look to the Internet to prove that we are important, valuable, and loved. And because we accept the presence of indwelling sin, we will not be blind to the potential idolatries and temptations we can succumb to online. And because we know ourselves to be fallen creatures, we will accept the limits of our human condition. We cannot have meaningful relationships with thousands of people. We cannot *really* know what is going on in the world. We cannot be truly here and there at the same time. The biggest deception of our digital age may be the lie that says we can be omni-competent, omni-informed, and omni-present. We cannot be any of these things. We must choose our absence, our inability, and our ignorance—and choose wisely. The sooner we embrace this finitude, the sooner we can be free.

8

Rhythm and Blues

Diagnosis #6: You'd Better Rest
Yourself before You Wreck Yourself

We came to the end of our weekly meeting, and I could tell that Jason had something uncomfortable to say. Jason is a good friend of mine and, along with Ben, he's one of the two best associate pastors a senior pastor could ever work with. We had gone through the agenda for over an hour when Jason told me he had one other thing he wanted to talk about.

"Kevin, are you taking your day off?"

I told him what my plan was and how the last couple of weeks were exceptionally hectic and full of surprises. Jason was sympathetic and the farthest thing from legalistic, but he pressed in a little further.

"You need to take a day off."

"I often do."

"Every week."

"Well, I was taking Mondays off, but now that my kids are in school I switched to Saturdays so I can spend the day with them. But sermon prep always spills over to Saturday. I've been trying to spend extra time at home a couple of mornings a week. And my schedule can be flexible to come home during lunch if I need to."

"You need a day off," my friend said to me one more time. "Whatever your theology of the Sabbath, you're not being smart. You can't keep this up."

"I know. I know. You're right. Something has to change."

The Sabbath Was Made for Man

Knowing what to believe about the Sabbath is harder than it looks. Some Christians believe little has changed relative to the fourth commandment, and Sunday is now a Christian Sabbath. Others argue that the Sabbath was fulfilled in Christ and now there is almost complete freedom in our weekly routines. A small minority of Christians believe Saturday is still the proper day for Sabbath rest and worship. Plenty has been written about these important differences.[1] Personally, I resonate with Greg Beale's three conclusions:

> First, the seventh-day commemoration in Gen. 2:3 and Israel's Sabbath ordinance is transferred to the first day of the week because of Christ's resurrection.
>
> Second, Israel's way of observing the Sabbath, with all its detailed requirements, falls away, and there is a return to

[1] See, for example: Christopher John Donato, ed., *Perspectives on the Sabbath: Four Views* (Nashville: B&H Academic, 2011); Iain D. Campbell, *On the First Day of the Week: God, the Christian, and the Sabbath* (Leominster, UK: DayOne, 2005); D. A. Carson, ed., *From Sabbath to Lord's Day: A Biblical, Historical, and Theological Investigation* (Eugene, OR: Wipf & Stock, 1982).

the creational mandate. The observance of this mandate is a day of commemoration of God's creative rest, a celebration that Christ has entered that rest, that believers have begun to enter such rest, and a pointing forward to believers completely entering that rest.

In addition, Christ's coming fulfills Israel's unique Sabbath commandment, since he is Israel's Messiah, accomplishing Israel's end-time exodus and representing true Israel and the end-time temple.[2]

Or to put it more simply, we should rest in Christ alone for our salvation. But along with that there is still an abiding principle that we ought to worship on the Lord's Day and trust God enough to have a weekly routine where we cease from our normal labors.[3] We need God's ordinary means on Sunday for our extraordinarily busy lives the rest of the week.

Whatever your take on the specific dos and don'ts of Sunday, I hope every Christian can agree that God has made us from the dust to need regular times of rest. He built it into the creation order and commanded it of his people. God's design was not to punish little kids with naps on Sundays or to drive us to boredom and inactivity once every seven days. He made the Sabbath for man, not man for the Sabbath (Mark 2:27). God gives us Sabbath as a gift; it's an island of get-to in a sea of have-to. He also offers us Sabbath as a test; it's an opportunity to trust God's work more than our own. When I go weeks without

---

[2] G. K. Beale, *A New Testament Biblical Theology: The Unfolding of the Old Testament in the New* (Grand Rapids, MI: Baker Academic, 2011), 800–801. Paragraph breaks are mine.
[3] For a further development of my theology of the fourth commandment, see Kevin DeYoung, *The Good News We Almost Forgot: Rediscovering the Gospel in a 16th Century Catechism* (Chicago: Moody, 2010), 178–182.

taking adequate time off, I may or may not be disobeying the fourth commandment, but I'm certainly too convinced of my own importance and more than a little foolish. If my goal is God-glorifying productivity over a lifetime of hard work, there are few things I need more than a regular rhythm of rest.

Ain't Got No Rhythm

It's easy to find people who think work is good and leisure is bad (i.e., you rest to work). You can also find people who think leisure is good and work is bad (i.e., you work to rest). But according to the Bible, both work and rest can be good if they are done to the glory of God.[4] The Bible commends hard work (Prov. 6:6–11; Matt. 25:14–30; 1 Thess. 2:9; 4:11–12; 2 Thess. 3:10) and it also extols the virtue of rest (Ex. 20:8–11; Deut. 5:12–15; Ps. 127:2). Both have their place. The hard part is putting them in the right places.

Many of us are less busy than we think, but life feels constantly overwhelming because our days and weeks and years have no rhythm. As we saw in the previous chapter, one of the dangers of technology is that work and rest blend together in a confusing mush. We never quite leave work when we're at home, so the next day we have a hard time getting back to work when we're at work. We have no routine, no order to our days. We are never completely "on" and never totally "off." So we dawdle on YouTube for twenty minutes at the office and then catch up on e-mails for forty minutes in front of the TV at home. Perhaps this arrangement works for some employers

---

[4] See Tim Chester, *The Busy Christian's Guide to Busyness* (Nottingham, England: Inter-Varsity Press, 2006), 25–34.

and may feel freeing for many employees. But over time most of us work less effectively, whether it's in the home or out of the home, and find our work less enjoyable when there is no regular, concentrated, deliberate break.

Not long ago, the *Wall Street Journal* ran a fascinating article about four-time Olympian Bernard Lagat.[5] A native of Kenya but now a US citizen, Lagat holds seven American track and field records, ranging from the 1,500 meters to the 5,000. According to the article, one of the secrets to his running is, actually, not running. After eleven months of intense training and competition, Lagat "puts his sneakers in the closet and pigs out for five weeks. No running. No sit-ups. He coaches his son's soccer team and gains 8 pounds." He's taken this long break every fall since 1999. Lagat says "rest is a good thing" and calls the month of inactivity "pure bliss." Even the best in the world need a break. In fact, they wouldn't be the best without one. Idleness is not a mere indulgence or vice. It is necessary to getting anything done.

People like to say life is a marathon, not a sprint, but it's actually more like a track workout. We run hard and then rest hard. We charge a hill and then chug some Gatorade. We do some stairs, then some 200s, and then a few 400s. In between, we rest. Without it, we'd never finish the workout. If we want to keep going, we have to learn how to stop. Just like the Israelites had in their calendar, we need downtime each day, and a respite each week, and seasons of refreshment throughout the year. We can't run incessantly and expect to run very well.

---

[5] Scott Cacciola, "The Secret to Running: Not Running," *Wall Street Journal*, September 20, 2012.

We may think that more work is the answer to our decreasing drive and goldfish-like attention span, but rest is often the antidote we really need. Sometimes the best preparation is a wandering, soul-enriching procrastination. Take a nap, throw the Frisbee, sing a song, and then write the paper. The land won't produce a harvest if it never lies fallow. We can't be "all in" all the time. Just think of the Israelite calendar. It had times for feasting and times for fasting. It was for their piety *and* their productivity that God put them on a predictable pattern filled with daily, weekly, monthly, seasonal, annual, and multi-year rhythms.

Which is why it's so concerning that our lives are getting more and more rhythm-less. We don't have healthy routines. We can't keep our feasting and fasting apart. Evening and morning have lost their feel. Sunday has lost its significance. Everything is blurred together. The faucet is a constant drip. Life becomes a malaise, until we can't take any more and spiral into illness, burnout, or depression. Jason confronted me the way he did because he didn't want me to go down that drain.

He Gives to His Beloved Sleep

Pursuing a pattern of work and rest means more than an annual retreat or a weekly Sabbath. It means quite practically a daily fight to get more sleep. When Proverbs talks about the sluggard lying on his bed, it has in mind the kind of person who would rather starve than strive, the person who would rather receive a handout than put his hands to work. The chastisement is not a warning to spend as little time as possible in bed. God made us to need sleep, and when we think we can survive without it, we not only spurn his gift (Ps. 127:2); we show our mistaken self-reliance.

We tend to assume it's always godlier to forgo sleep for more important activity, but God made us physical beings. We can't go without sleep very long without doing our bodies and souls great damage. That's the way God made us—finite and fragile. He made us to spend almost a third of our lives not doing anything except depending on him. Going to sleep is our way of saying, "I trust you, God. You'll be okay without me." We regale each other with stories of great saints who got up at four or five o'clock in the morning to pray, forgetting that in the days before electricity most people went to bed soon after dark and woke up earlier in the morning. Most of our heroes from bygone ages probably slept much more than we do. Very few of us can survive, let alone thrive, on four or five hours a night.

By all accounts, we are sleeping less than ever before. The average American gets two and a half fewer hours of sleep per night than a century ago.[6] According to the Center for Disease Control and Prevention, more than 40 million Americans get fewer than six hours of sleep per night.[7] Though we often brag about how little sleep we get, studies show sleep deprivation is a trigger for problems like diabetes and obesity.[8] In today's world, with no environmental cues to force us to bed, and plenty of gadgets to keep us awake, we simply aren't getting the sleep we need.

---

[6] Richard A. Swenson, *Margin: Restoring Emotional, Physical, Financial, and Time Reserves to Overloaded Lives* (Colorado Springs: NavPress, 2004), 96.

[7] David. K. Randall, "Rethinking Sleep," *New York Times*, September 22, 2012.

[8] Mitch Leslie, "Sleep Study Suggests Triggers for Diabetes and Obesity," *Science* 335 (April 13, 2012): 143.

And yet, natural limitations cannot be transgressed without consequence. You can borrow time, but you can't steal it. If you have to finish a paper by eight o'clock in the morning you can wait till the last minute and stay up all night to finish it, and it may seem like a brilliant move. After all, what were you going to do with the hours between midnight and morning anyway? You were just going to waste it in bed. So now your paper is done and all you missed was one night's sleep. Good move, you!

But all you've really done is borrow time. You haven't gained any. Because you stayed up all night on Thursday, you'll invariably crash on Friday. If not on Friday, you'll sleep an extra five hours on Saturday. If you don't catch up on sleep over the weekend, you'll likely get sick the next week. And if you don't get sick and you keep pushing yourself on empty, your productivity will slide. Or you'll get into a car accident when you are beyond exhaustion. Or you'll snap at your friend and cause a relational meltdown that takes weeks to mend. The time you thought you stole cannot be so easily filched. You cannot cheat sleep indefinitely. And the longer you try to borrow against sleep, the more your body (or God) will force you to pay for those hours—plus interest.

When I read D. A. Carson's sermon on religious doubt a few years ago, I was struck that one of his six possible causes for doubt was "sleep deprivation." Here's one of the best scholars in the world telling us that we may be spiritually obligated to take a nap! Don't ignore his counsel:

> If you keep burning the candle at both ends, sooner or later
> you will indulge in more and more mean cynicism—and

the line between cynicism and doubt is a very thin one. Of course, different individuals require different numbers of hours of sleep; moreover, some cope with a bit of tiredness better than others. Nevertheless, if you are among those who become nasty, cynical, or even full of doubt when you are missing your sleep, you are morally obligated to try to get the sleep you need. We are whole, complicated beings: our physical existence is tied up to our spiritual well-being, to our mental outlook, to our relationships with others, including our relationship with God. Sometimes the godliest thing you can do in the universe is get a good night's sleep—not pray all night, but sleep. I'm certainly not denying that there may be a place for praying all night; I'm merely insisting that in the normal course of things, spiritual discipline obligates you to get the sleep your body needs.[9]

I know sleep is easier said than done, especially for parents with young children and those with insomnia, but most of us could improve our lives significantly by simply getting to bed a little earlier. Some nights I can't help it; there's no way to be in bed before midnight. But on other nights I get started on a project I didn't need to begin, or fritter away thirty minutes on my phone, or waste an extra forty-five minutes watching a meaningless sporting event, or spend an hour reading late at night instead of guarding that time so that I can get up to read my Bible the next morning. If we really paid attention, we'd be surprised to see what we do and don't do from eight to twelve o'clock every night. Maybe the culprit is dessert or caffeine or Facebook. Maybe we need to cut back on an evening

---

[9] D. A. Carson, *Scandalous: The Cross and the Resurrection of Jesus* (Wheaton, IL: Crossway, 2010), 147.

commitment. I can't make the hard decisions for you. But I know I need to make changes in my life, too. I can't make sleep deprivation a way of life. I can't make midnight the new eleven if I still want to get up at six thirty. Most of us have a tremendous sleep debt to pay, and the sooner we start banking those regular deposits the better—better for your work, better for your soul, and better for the ones you love.

The Hard Work of Rest

If this chapter on rest seems like hard work, that's because it is. It's hard to trust God, hard to let go, and hard to stop. When thinking about busyness, people talk as if hard work is the problem. But we're not actually in danger of working too hard. We simply work hard at things in the wrong proportions. If you work eighty hours a week and never see your kids and never talk to your wife, people may call you a workaholic. And no doubt you're putting a lot of effort into your career. But you may not be working very hard at being a dad or being a husband or being a man after God's own heart.

We all know we need rest from work, but we don't realize we have to work hard just to rest. We have to plan for breaks. We have to schedule time to be unscheduled. That's the way life is for most of us. Scattered, frantic, boundary-less busyness comes naturally. The rhythms of work and rest require planning.

More than that, they require godly habits. I have never had trouble finding time for our Sunday worship services. Not once. I'm never double-booked during those times. I never feel pressure to say yes to another request or squeeze in another appointment at eleven o'clock Sunday morning. Why? Because it's a habit, has been my whole life. I go to church on Sunday. It's there. It's fixed. I've planned for it. The day may be full, but there is a comfortable routine. I get up, read my Bible, pray, look at my sermon, eat breakfast, go to church, pray, preach, preach again, talk to people, go home, eat lunch, take a nap, look at my sermon, go back to church. The rhythm gives me purpose and order. It gives me life.

I can't make it through Sunday without a rhythm. I won't make it far in life without one, either. There must be times when I won't work; otherwise I won't rest. And there must be times I have to sleep, or I will keep borrowing what I can't repay. I'm not so important in God's universe that I can't afford to rest. But my God-given limitations are so real that I can't afford not to.

9

Embracing the Burdens of Busyness

Diagnosis #7: You Suffer More because You Don't Expect to Suffer at All

After several chapters with lists of 10 or 7 or 3 (at least they weren't 40 or 144,000!) let me start this chapter by getting right to the conclusion: *the reason we are busy is because we are supposed to be busy.*

This may seem like a strange way to (almost) end a book on busyness. But keep in mind that this is the last of seven diagnoses, not the only one. If this were the only point of the book you'd think, "Great, life is going to stink! I'm supposed to feel overwhelmed. I should be neglecting family and strung out on four asleep. Super! I guess I'll sign the kids up for tae kwon do." I wrote the rest of this book because that's not the way we should feel. Busyness is a big problem. It comes with serious spiritual dangers. There's a reason this chapter is not the only chapter in the book.

And there's a reason it's one of the chapters. I don't want you to think the best thing we can do for ourselves and for the world is to take a pass on every difficult request, live for leisure, and throw ourselves a giant "me party." I don't want you to think that hard work is the problem, or that sacrificing for others is the problem, or that suffering is necessarily the problem. If you have creativity, ambition, and love, you will be busy. We are supposed to disciple the nations. We are supposed to work with our hands. We are supposed to love God with our minds. We are supposed to have babies and take care of them. It's not a sin to be busy. It's not wrong to be active.

Busyness, as I've been diagnosing it, is as much a mind-set and a heart sickness as it is a failure in time management. It's possible to live your days in a flurry of hard work, serving, and bearing burdens, and to do so with the right character and a right dependence on God so that it doesn't feel crazy busy. By the same token, it's possible to feel amazingly stressed and frenzied while actually accomplishing very little. The antidote to busyness of soul is not sloth and indifference. The antidote is rest, rhythm, death to pride, acceptance of our own finitude, and trust in the providence of God.

The busyness that's bad is not the busyness of work, but the busyness that works hard at the wrong things. It's being busy trying to please people, busy trying to control others, busy trying to do things we haven't been called to do. So please don't hear from me that work is bad or that bearing burdens is bad. That's part of life. That's part of being a Christian. When Tim Kreider, writing in the *New York Times*, says, "The Puritans turned work into a virtue, evidently forgetting that God invented it as a punishment,"[1] he's wrong about the Puritans and wrong about God. We were made to cultivate the Garden of God, to replenish the earth and subdue it. The pains and the thorns were curses, but not work itself. We were made to be busy.

To Serve Is to Suffer

One of the reasons we struggle so mightily with busyness is because we do not expect to struggle. Many Western Christians—and I'm chief among them—can easily live with the tacit assumption that we should not suffer. Sure, we might get cancer someday. We might lose our job for a season. Maybe we'll get one of those terrifying calls in the middle of the night. Those are dreadful losses. But day in and day out we don't expect to suffer. And the less we expect to suffer, the more devastating suffering becomes.

We simply don't think of our busyness as even a *possible* part of our cross to bear. But what if mothering small children isn't supposed to be easy? What if pastoring a congregation is supposed to be challenging? What if being a friend, or just being a Christian, is supposed to mean a lot of time-consuming, burden-bearing, gloriously busy, and wildly inefficient work?

In his excellent article "To Serve Is to Suffer," Ajith Fernando writes about using our gifts "in the fog of fatigue."[2] He explains how people often sympathize with him for serving in

---

[1] Tim Kreider, "The 'Busy' Trap," *New York Times*, June 30, 2012.
[2] Ajith Fernando, "To Serve Is to Suffer," *Christianity Today* (August 2010), at http://www.christianitytoday.com/globalconversation/august2010/.

a country like Sri Lanka, a country wracked by war and hostile to evangelism. And he admits that ministry there can be very hard. One of his ministry's staff workers was brutally assaulted and killed. But the greatest suffering has come from the people he works with: "Whether you live in the East or the West," Fernando says, "you will suffer if you are committed to people."

Then he tells a story that ought to make those of us from the "developed world" sit up and take note:

> I have a large group of people to whom I write asking for prayer when I have a need. Sometimes my need is overcoming tiredness. When I write about this, many write back saying they are praying that God would strengthen me and guide me in my scheduling. However, there are differences in the way friends from the East and some from the West respond. I get the strong feeling that many in the West think struggling with tiredness from overwork is evidence of disobedience to God. My contention is that it is wrong if one gets sick from overwork through drivenness and insecurity. But we may have to endure tiredness when we, like Paul, are servants of people.

Let that sink in and then read one more paragraph:

> The West, having struggled with the tyrannical rule of time, has a lot to teach the East about the need for rest. The East has something to teach the West about embracing physical problems that come from commitment to people. If you think it is wrong to suffer physically because of ministry, then you suffer more from the problem than those who believe that suffering is an inevitable step on the path to fruitfulness and fulfillment.

When I first read that a couple of years ago I had to stop, and think, and then repent. How quick I am to feel sorry for myself. How quick to assume I shouldn't have to bear any heavy burdens. How quick to conclude that God could never want me to struggle with tiredness or sickness for the sake of others. I understand, coming toward the end of the book, I run the risk of undermining all the necessary warnings and prescriptions that have come before. I trust you are discerning enough to know this chapter does not negate all the others. But I know from personal experience that some forms of busyness are from the Lord and bring him glory. Effective love is rarely efficient. People take time. Relationships are messy. If we love others, how can we not be busy and burdened at least some of the time?

No matter how well we plan or how much we get re-energized from a Sabbath or a vacation, there are bound to be times where life feels overwhelming. While working on this book, I enjoyed many days of relative calm, without many pressures in my schedule. But as soon as I went back to work everything hit me again—all at once. This is what it's like for any of us coming back from a break. The day after I returned from my study leave I had an elders' meeting, a meeting with our pastoral interns, a meeting with an engaged couple to plan their wedding, and a last-minute funeral—plus all the regular e-mails and phone calls and a sermon to write. After weeks of ruminating about busyness, suddenly I was tremendously busy again. Nothing in this book could have prevented the busyness of returning to work, but it helped to remember that busyness isn't always bad and can't always be avoided. Momma said there'd be days like this.

Apostolic Anxiety

Second Corinthians 11:28 always seemed like a strange verse to me. Until I became a pastor.[3] Here's Paul rattling off all the ways he's been beaten up for Jesus—imprisonments, lashes, rods, stoning, being shipwrecked and adrift at sea, sleepless nights, hunger and thirst, cold and exposure, danger from everyone everywhere (vv. 23–27)—and then, as the cherry on top, Paul mentions one more trial: "apart from other things, there is the daily pressure on me of my anxiety for all the churches" (v. 28). This is the mighty apostle Paul, the one who counted it a joy to "spend and be spent" for his people (12:15), the one who was sorrowful yet always rejoicing (6:10). This is the Paul who faced every imaginable opposition and yet learned to be content (Phil. 4:11) and anxious about nothing (4:6). And here he is admitting that, even with everything else he's endured, he still feels daily pressure and anxiety for all the churches.

Ever since becoming a pastor, I have found unusual comfort in this verse. It's not that I have accomplished what Paul accomplished, or suffered what he suffered, but every earnest minister will feel this burden for the church. And Paul had several churches to burden him! Even if you're not a pastor, you know what Paul is talking about. He's talking about the pain of human relationships. The early Christian communities (like our Christian communities) were full of infighting and backbiting. They had to deal with false teaching. They were prone to legalism on one end and complete chaos on the other. Some of the church members were making insignificant matters too

---

[3] This last section is adapted from my article "Pastoral Pressure and Apostolic Anxiety," *Tabletalk*, August 2011.

important, while others were too willing to compromise on Christian essentials. Paul loved these churches, and their struggles burdened him more than shipwreck or imprisonment.

I'm not surprised that Paul felt daily pressure. His work never seemed to let up. He had letters to write, visits to make, a collection to gather for the church in Jerusalem. He had to send people here and there and manage the affairs of his churches from a distance. He had to respond to a myriad of criticisms, often conflicting criticisms. Some people thought he was too harsh. Others said he was too weak. Some people in his churches were ascetics and thought Paul was worldly. Others were licentious and thought Paul was too ethically demanding. They complained about his teaching. They questioned his credentials. They compared him negatively to the original apostles. They thought him lame compared to the false apostles. They didn't like the way he handled money. They didn't like his preaching style. They didn't like the way he arranged his travel plans. They didn't like his discipline. On some days they just didn't like Paul anymore. All this for the man who led them to Christ, loved them like a father, planted their church, refused their money, and risked his neck for their spiritual good. There was no weight for Paul like the weight of caring for God's people.

Paul was busy, in all the right ways. If you love God and serve others, you will be busy too. Sometimes we will get frazzled. We will feel pressure. We will be tired. We will get discouraged. We will feel exhausted. We will say, "Who is weak, and I am not weak?" (2 Cor. 11:29). But be encouraged. God uses weak things to shame the strong (1 Cor. 1:27). His grace is sufficient for you; his power is made perfect in weakness (2 Cor. 12:9). For the sake of Christ, we must be content with weaknesses, insults, hardships, persecutions, and calamities. And yes, sometimes we must be content with busyness. For when you are weak, then you are strong (v. 10). Paul had pressure. You have pressure too. But God can handle the pressure. Do not be surprised when you face crazy weeks of all kinds. And do not be surprised when God sustains you in the midst of them.

10

The One Thing You Must Do

The problem with a book on busyness is that busy people read it. So there's a good possibility you haven't made it all the way to chapter 10. And if you have, you are now hoping for a big payoff: a great five-point plan to simplify your life; a brilliant ten-point manifesto on restoring sanity to your world; a simple twelve-step program to becoming a less hectic you in forty days.

Well, for better or worse—actually better, I think—I don't have a self-help makeover to offer. I can't fix your broken, busy life. I'm having enough trouble dealing with my own. But what I can give you is one thing you absolutely must do. Think of it as a one-point plan with no guaranteed results.

Except that it will bring you closer to Jesus.

Which, come to think of it, is positively the best way to handle your busyness.

A Martha Work Ethic in a Lazy Mary World!

At the end of Luke 10 we find the closest thing Jesus gave to a sermon on busyness. The whole story is only a paragraph in most Bibles, and Jesus's part is only two sentences. But maybe this is because busy people can't handle long sermons. In any event, it was the right message at the time, and it's the right message for us today:

> Now as they went on their way, Jesus entered a village. And a woman named Martha welcomed him into her house. And she had a sister called Mary, who sat at the Lord's feet and listened to his teaching. But Martha was distracted with much serving. And she went up to him and said, "Lord, do you not care that my sister has left me to serve alone? Tell her then to help me." But the Lord answered her, "Martha, Martha, you are anxious and troubled about many things, but one thing is necessary. Mary has chosen the good portion, which will not be taken away from her." (Luke 10:38–42)

No matter how many times I read this story I always sympathize with Martha. I want to enter the scene and protest, "But, Jesus, how can you encourage such irresponsibility? There's a time for teaching and for learning, and this is not it. The house is going to be a mess and no one will get their supper if you let everyone worship and pray and sit at your feet instead of cleaning and serving."

Of course, I don't usually make those thoughts public. I know Mary is supposed to be our example here, not Martha. But I just can't help feeling like Jesus is not being very realistic. Somebody has to get this stuff done. We can't be reading books or listening to sermons all day. I'm a pastor, and I can't even do that. My family needs me. The church, the government, my friends—they all expect me to stay on top of things. Mary's style might work for a monk or a personal retreat day, but her little time-out simply isn't doable as a way of life.

Besides, Martha was doing important things. It's not like she was glued to her phone, watching kittens breakdance. She was serving, just as the Bible says (Rom. 12:7; 1 Pet. 4:11). We need *Martha*s. We need servants. We need people who love to work hard. Someone has to do the dishes. Someone has to stack the chairs. Someone has to set the table and preheat the oven so that the *Mary*s of the world can have their spiritual epiphanies.

Good, Better, Best

That's what Martha was feeling. That's how many of us feel. And that's perfectly understandable. It's just not the way Jesus sees things. Martha implores Jesus to do something (Luke 10:40). She thinks, "Surely Jesus will see what is going on here. Surely the one who came to serve others will see all the trouble Mary is causing me. Surely Jesus will get my back."

But then he doesn't.

He starts by saying her name, twice. The repetition speaks of intense emotion, like "Master, Master . . . !" (Luke 8:24), or "O Jerusalem, Jerusalem . . . !" (13:34), or "Simon, Simon . . ." (22:31). It's possible Jesus was upset: "Martha! Martha!!" But I suspect he was more gentle and soothing. John 11:5 says, "Jesus loved Martha and her sister and Lazarus." Jesus loved this whole family. Martha was a kind lady who was generous to her guests and took her hospitality seriously. I don't think Jesus was fuming. He just wants his friend to see what her sister sees.

"Martha, Martha," he says, "you are anxious and troubled about many things." The NIV says she was "worried and upset." The Message says "Martha, dear Martha, you're fussing far too much and getting yourself worked up over nothing." Many of us can relate. We go day after day, crazy month after crazy month: worried, upset, anxious, troubled, fussing, worked up. Every stain, every school project, every dirty sink, every surprise guest, every surge of responsibility becomes a cause for great panic. To paraphrase Titus 3:3, we live as slaves to various passions and pleasures, passing our days in chaos and envy, hassled by others and hassling one another. We are all very busy, but not with what matters most.

That's the crux of the story: "Martha, you are freaking out, but only one thing is needed. Mary has chosen the good portion. She is sitting at my feet to learn and to worship. I'm not going to take that away from her. Your busyness is not wrong. But it is not best." Granted, we shouldn't take this episode as a blueprint for every moment of every day. If God expected us to do nothing but sit cross-legged on the floor and journal, the Bible could have been much smaller. Mary's example is not a summons to the contemplative life in a cloister. But it's a pretty strong reminder that we had better keep first things first.

For my money, the most important word in the whole story is "distracted" in verse 40. Martha isn't doing anything bad. She's just being pulled away from what is better. She's so busy with dinner that she's giving Jesus her spiritual leftovers. Personally, I have the palate of a four-year-old and don't like most food the first time around. And I really don't care for leftovers. But that's what we give to God when we don't keep first things first. He's not glaring at us from heaven when we have a hectic day. And yet, he knows that we are missing out on "the good portion." It is not enough to let "God-stuff" fill in the cracks during the day. Sitting at the feet of Jesus, whether corporately or individually, never just happens. We must make learning from him and taking time to be with him a priority.

The priority, in fact. If someone recorded your life for a week and then showed it to a group of strangers, what would they guess is the "good portion" in your life? What would they conclude is the one thing you must get done every day? Folding the laundry? Cleaning the house? Catching up on e-mails? Posting to Facebook? Mowing the lawn? Watching the game? I know you have things to do. I have plenty to do myself. But out of all the concerns in our lives, can we honestly say *and show* that sitting at the feet of Jesus is the one thing that is necessary?

That's Why They're Called Devotions

If you are sick and tired of feeling so dreadfully busy and are looking for a one-point plan to help restore order to your life, this is the best advice I know: devote yourself to the Word of God and prayer. This means public worship and private worship. I'm not telling you how much time to spend. You may start with five minutes a day or fifteen or fifty. A few unhurried minutes are better than a distracted hour, and a consistent habit is better than a sporadic burst of fits and starts. As someone who has had a devotional time since high school—and has also struggled to have a devotional time since high school—I can tell you that no single practice brings more peace and discipline to life than sitting at the feet of Jesus.

I understand that ending this book in this way is a dangerous and potentially debilitating move. The pursuit of personal devotions is one of the strongholds of legalism. Anytime we talk about what we should do every day, we must make clear what Christ has already done for us. We can rest, because he worked. We can lay down our prideful busyness, because he laid down his life. We can keep coming back to him in the midst of our failures, because he keeps all his promises to us. The last thing I want to do is to lay down a law that says you must read through the Bible in a year or the Lord will smite you in his wrath.

And yet, few things demonstrate our devotion to Christ more than making time with him a priority each day. As J. C. Ryle observed, "A man may preach from false motives. A man may write books, and make fine speeches, and seem diligent in good works, and yet be a Judas Iscariot. But a man seldom goes into his closet, and pours out his soul before God in secret, unless he is serious." People know if you pray at the dinner table. They know if you attend worship on Sunday. They know if you are part of a small group. But they don't know if you are finding desolate places to pray.[1]

Like many of you, I often look at my busy life and don't know where to start. I wish I exercised more, and ate better, and kept track of my receipts, and programmed the presets in my car, and had my files in order, and knew where those little thingies for the basketball pump were, and in general didn't feel like I was walking on the knife edge of craziness all the time. My temptation is to tackle everything at once. Or nothing at all. But the best plan is to start with Jesus's plan.

God has given us all twenty-four hours in every day. It is

---

[1] J. C. Ryle, *A Call to Prayer*. Accessed January 17, 2013, at http://www.gracegems.org/Ryle /a_call_to_prayer.htm.

the one resource distributed with complete equality. And for most of us, for the most part, we all do with those hours what we think is most important. I wish I ran more, but apparently I value reading at home, or working late, or getting sleep more. So the answer here is not simple willpower: "I must spend more time with Jesus!" That won't last. We have to believe that hearing from God is our good portion. We have to believe that the most significant opportunity before us every day is the opportunity to sit at the feet of Jesus. We won't rearrange our priorities unless we really believe this is the best one.

In his book *The Power of Habit*, Charles Duhigg argues that people usually change bad habits most effectively by focusing on only one pattern, or what Duhigg calls a "keystone habit."[2] You don't have to buy everything in Duhigg's book to see the wisdom in this suggestion. If we concentrate on one specific habit, instead of on the thousand areas that make up our busy lives, we are more likely to be successful, not just in that one area but in many others. For example, think of what could happen if you made it your one firm, resolute goal to spend time every day in the Word of God and prayer. You'd probably decide you need to get to bed earlier so you have time in the morning to read and pray (or so that you don't fall asleep later in the day). And because you want to get to bed earlier, you'd be more careful about what you eat late at night. And you would think twice before watching a show you had no intention of watching or rummaging around the Internet for thirty minutes for nothing in particular. And maybe you'd feel

[2] Charles Duhigg, *The Power of Habit: Why We Do What We Do in Life and Business* (New York: Random House, 2012), xiv, 97–126.

less stressed about leaving the house a bit disheveled because you knew you were choosing the better part by sitting at the feet of Jesus. And maybe you'd allow yourself to ignore those after-work e-mails, or simply put the screens away altogether. Who knows how many little distractions you might set aside in an effort to be more Mary than Martha?

And that's not even taking into account the spiritual benefits. By spending time with the Lord in the Word and prayer, we are likely to gain new perspective on our hassles and headaches. Starting each day with eternity makes our petty problems and long to-do lists seem less significant. By sitting at the feet of Jesus, we will grow more like him—more patient, more loving, more thoughtful. We'll see that our screens do not satisfy like our Savior. We'll see that wisdom was not born yesterday, or thirty-four seconds ago on social media. We'll learn to keep our complaints to a minimum and our eyes on the cross. And we'll become more helpful to those around us. What Paul Tripp says about pastoral ministry is true for everyone's ministry: "I am more and more convinced that what gives a ministry its motivations, perseverance, humility, joy, tenderness, passion, and grace is the devotional life of the one doing ministry. When I daily admit how needy I am, daily mediate on the grace of the Lord Jesus Christ, and daily feed on the restorative wisdom of his Word, I am propelled to share with others the grace that I am daily receiving at the hands of my Savior."[3] Maybe devotion to Christ really is the one thing that is necessary.

---

[3] Paul Tripp, *Dangerous Calling: Confronting the Unique Challenges of Pastoral Ministry* (Wheaton, IL: Crossway, 2012), 35.

The Life We Want Is the Life We Need

I hope you can tell that this book has been for me as much as for anyone. I am a driven person. I have a high sense of responsibility and obligation. I don't like letting people down. I don't like leaving things undone. I don't like being late. I wake up in the morning with my motor running. I talk a lot about Mary sorts of things because I know I'm wired as a Martha. And so are most of you. We hate being busy. But we may never hate it enough to change. The bane of busyness must be fought with stronger stuff.

Have you ever noticed everything else that happens in Luke 10 before we get to Mary and Martha? Jesus sends out seventy-two disciples on a mission trip. They heal the sick, cast out demons, and preach the gospel. Jesus thought the trip was so successful that he said he saw Satan fall like lightning from heaven (v. 18). Then later in chapter 10, Jesus tells the parable of the Good Samaritan, the man who showed compassion to a stranger, loved his neighbor, and inconvenienced himself for the good of his fellow man. Do you see how Luke places the story of Mary and Martha after all this activity? This episode isn't here by accident. I believe God wants us to see that if we heal the sick and cast out demons and preach the gospel and show mercy and do justice and don't sit at the feet of Jesus, we've missed the one thing we truly need. The only thing more important than ministry is being ministered to.

Making consistent time for the Word of God and prayer is the place to start because being with Jesus is the only thing strong enough to pull us away from busyness. Luke 10:38–42 is nothing but a story version of Deuteronomy 8:3: "Man does not live by bread alone, but . . . by every word that comes from the mouth of the LORD." We won't say no to more craziness until we can say yes to more Jesus. We will keep choosing dinner rolls over the bread of life. We will choose the fanfare of the world over the feet of Jesus. We will choose busyness over blessing.

It's not wrong to be tired. It's not wrong to feel overwhelmed. It's not wrong to go through seasons of complete chaos. What is wrong—and heartbreakingly foolish and wonderfully avoidable—is to live a life with more craziness than we want because we have less Jesus than we need.

General Index

Scripture Index

DOWNLOAD THE
FREE STUDY GUIDE

CrazyBusyBook.com